HAS FREEDOM
A FUTURE?

HAS FREEDOM A FUTURE?

Adolph Lowe

CONVERGENCE

A Series Founded, Planned, and Edited
by Ruth Nanda Anshen

PRAEGER

New York
Westport, Connecticut
London

Library of Congress Cataloging-in-Publication Data

Lowe, Adolph, 1893–
    Has freedom a future? / Adolph Lowe.
        p.   cm.—(Convergence)
    Bibliography: p.
    Includes index.
    ISBN 0-275-92937-X (alk. paper)
    ISBN 0-275-92938-8 (pbk. : alk. paper)
    1. Liberty.   2. Liberalism—Great Britain.   3. Liberalism—United
States.   4. Welfare state.   I. Title.   II. Series: Convergence (New
York, N.Y.)
JC585.L67 1988
323.44—dc19   87-29943

Library of Congress Catalog Card Number: 87-29943
ISBN: 0-275-92937-X
        0-275-92938-8 (pbk.)

First published in 1988

Praeger Publishers, One Madison Avenue, New York, NY 10010
A division of Greenwood Press, Inc.

Printed in the United States of America

The paper used in this book complies with the
Permanent Paper Standard issued by the National
Information Standards Organization (Z39.48-1984).

10 9 8 7 6 5 4 3 2 1

To Robert L. Heilbroner

CONVERGENCE

A Series Founded, Planned, and Edited by Ruth Nanda Anshen

Board of Editors

BOOKS IN THE CONVERGENCE SERIES

Contents

Convergence

Ruth Nanda Anshen

"There is no use trying," said Alice; "one *can't* believe impossible things."

"I dare say you haven't had much practice," said the Queen, "When I was your age, I always did it for half an hour a day. Why, sometimes I've believed as many as six impossible things before breakfast."

This commitment is an inherent part of human nature and an aspect of our creativity. Each advance of science brings increased comprehension and appreciation of the nature, meaning, and wonder of the creative forces that move the cosmos and created man. Such openness and confidence lead to faith in the reality of possibility and eventually to the following truth: "The mystery of the universe is its comprehensibility."

When Einstein uttered that challenging statement, he could have been speaking about our relationship with the universe. The old division of the Earth and the Cosmos into objective processes in space and time and mind in which they are mirrored is no longer a suitable starting point for understanding the universe, science, or ourselves. Science now begins to focus on the convergence of man and nature, on the framework which makes us, as living beings, dependent parts of nature and simultaneously makes nature the object of our thoughts and actions. Scientists can no longer confront the universe as objective observers. Science recognizes the participation of man with the universe. Speaking quantitatively, the uni-

verse is largely indifferent to what happens in man. Speaking qual-
itatively, nothing happens in man that does not have a bearing on
the elements which constitute the universe. This gives cosmic significance to the person.

Nevertheless, all facts are not born free and equal. There exists
a hierarchy of facts in relation to a hierarchy of values. To arrange
the facts rightly, to differentiate the important from the trivial, to
see their bearing in relation to each other and to evaluational criteria, requires a judgment which is intuitive as well as empirical. We
need meaning in addition to information. Accuracy is not the same
as truth.

Our hope is to overcome the cultural *hubris* in which we have
been living. The scientific method, the technique of analyzing, ex-
plaining, and classifying, has demonstrated its inherent limitations.
They arise because, by its intervention, science presumes to alter
and fashion the object of its investigation. In reality, method and
object can no longer be separated. The outworn Cartesian, scientific world view has ceased to be scientific in the most profound
sense of the word, for a common bond links us all—man, animal,
plant, and galaxy—in the unitary principle of all reality. For the
self without the universe is empty.

This universe of which we human beings are particles may be
defined as a living, dynamic process of unfolding. It is a breathing
universe, its respiration being only one of the many rhythms of its
life. It is evolution itself. Although what we observe may seem to
be a community of separate, independent units, in actuality these
units are made up of subunits, each with a life of its own, and the
subunits constitute smaller living entities. At no level in the hierarchy of nature is independence a reality. For that which lives and
constitutes matter, whether organic or inorganic, is dependent on
discrete entities that, gathered together, form aggregates of new
units which interact in support of one another and become an unfolding event, in constant motion, with ever-increasing complexity
and intricacy of their organization.

Are there goals in evolution? Or are there only discernible patterns? Certainly there is a law of evolution by which we can explain the emergence of forms capable of activities which are indeed
novel. Examples may be said to be the origin of life, the emergence
of individual consciousness, and the appearance of language.

The hope of the concerned authors in Convergence is that they will show that evolution and development are interchangeable and that the entire system of the interweaving of man, nature, and the universe constitutes a living totality. Man is searching for his legitimate place in this unity, this cosmic scheme of things. The meaning of this cosmic scheme—if indeed we can impose meaning on the mystery and majesty of nature—and the extent to which we can assume responsibility in it as uniquely intelligent beings, are supreme questions for which this Series seeks an answer.

Inevitably, toward the end of a historial period, when thought and custom have petrified into rigidity and when the elaborate machinery of civilization opposes and represses our more noble qualities, life stirs again beneath the hard surface. Nevertheless, this attempt to define the purpose of Convergence is set forth with profound trepidation. We are living in a period of extreme darkness. There is moral atrophy, destructive radiation within us, as we watch the collapse of values hitherto cherished—but now betrayed. We seem to be face to face with an apocalyptic destiny. The anomie, the chaos, surrounding us produces an almost lethal disintegration of the person, as well as ecological and demographic disaster. Our situation is desperate. And there is no glossing over the deep and unresolved tragedy that fills our lives. Science now begins to question its premises and tells us not only what *is*, but what *ought* to be; *pre*scribing in addition to *de*scribing the realities of life, reconciling order and hierarchy.

My introduction to Convergence is not to be construed as a prefatory essay to each individual volume. These few pages attempt to set forth the general aim and purpose of this Series. It is my hope that this statement will provide the reader with a new orientation in his thinking, one more specifically defined by these scholars who hae been invited to participate in this intellectual, spiritual, and moral endeavor so desperately needed in our time. These scholars recognize the relevance of the nondiscursive experience of life which the discursive, analytical method alone is unable to convey.

The authors invited to Convergence Series acknowledge a structural kinship between subject and object, betrween living and nonliving matter, the immanence of the past energizing the present and thus bestowing a promise for the future. This kinship has long been sensed and experienced by mystics. Saint Francis of Assisi described with extraordinary beauty the truth that the more we know about nature, its unity with all life, the more we realize that we are one family, summoned to acknowledge the intimacy of our familial ties with the universe. At one time we were so anthropomorphic as to exclude as inferior such other aspects of our relatives as animals, plants, galaxies, or other species—even inorganic matter. This only exposed our provincialism. Then we believed there were borders beyond which we could not, must not, trespass. These frontiers have never existed. Now we are beginning to recognize, even take pride in, our neighbors in the Cosmos.

Human thought has been formed through centuries of man's consciousness, by perceptions and meanings that relate us to nature. The smallest living entity, be it a molecule or a particle, is at the same time present in the structure of the Earth and all its inhabitants, whether human or manifesting themselves in the multiplicity of other forms of life.

Today we are beginning to open ourselves to this evolved experience of consciousness. We keenly realize that man has intervened in the evolutionary process. The future is contingent, not completely prescribed, except for the immediate necessity to evaluate in order to live a life of integrity. The specific gravity of the burden of change has moved from genetic to cultural evolution. Genetic evolution itself has taken millions of years; cultural evolution is a child of no more than twenty or thirty thousand years. What will be the future of our evolutionary course? Will it be cyclical in the classical sense? Will it be linear in the modern sense? Yet we know that the laws of nature are not linear. Certainly, life is more than mere endless repetition. We must restore the importance of each moment, each deed. This is impossible if the future is nothing but a mechanical extrapolation of the past. Dignity becomes possible only with choice. The choice is ours.

In this light, evolution shows man arisen by a creative power inherent in the universe. The immense ancestral effort that has borne man invests him with a cosmic responsibility. Michelangelo's image of Adam created at God's command becomes a more intelligent symbol of man's position in the world than does a description of man as a chance aggregate of atoms or cells. Each successive stage of emergence is more comprehensive, more meaningful, more fulfilling, and more converging, than the last. Yet a higher faculty must always operate through the levels that are below it. The higher faculty must enlist the laws controlling the lower levels in the service of higher principles, and the lower level which enables the higher one to operate through it will always limit the scope of these operations, even menacing them with possible failure. All our higher endeavors must work through our lower forms and are necessarily exposed thereby to corruption. We may thus recognize the cosmic roots of tragedy and our fallible human condition. Language itself as the power of universals, is the basic expression of man's ability to transcend his environment and to transmute tragedy into a moral and spiritual triumph.

This relationship, this convergence, of the higher with the lower applies again when an upper level, such as consciousness or freedom, endeavors to reach beyond itself. If no higher level can be accounted for by the operation of a lower level, then no effort of ours an be truly creative in the sense of establishing a higher principle not intrinsic to our initial condition. And establishing such a principle is what all great art, great thought, and great action must aim at. This is indeed how these efforts have built up the heritage in which our lives continue to grow.

Has man's intelligence broken through the limits of his own powers? Yes and no. Inventive efforts can never fully account for their success, but the story of man's evolution testifies to a reative power that goes beyond that which we can account for in ourselves. This power can make us surpass ourselves. We exercise some of it in the simple act of acquiring knowledge and holding it to be true. For, in doing so, we strive for intellectual control over things outside ourselves, in spite of our manifest incapacity to justify this hope. The greatest efforts of the human mind amount to no more than this. All such acts impose an obligation to strive for the ostensibly impossible, representing man's search for the fulfillment of those ideals which, for the moment, seem to be beyond his reach. For the good of a moral act is inherent in the act itself and has the power to ennoble the person who performs it. Without this moral ingredient there is corruption.

The origins of one person can be envisaged by tracing that person's family tree all the way back to the primeval specks of protoplasm in which his first origins lie. The history of the family tree converges with everything that has contributed to the making of a human being. This segment of evolution is on a par with the history of a fertilized egg developing into a mature person, or the history of a plant growing from a seed; it includes everything that caused that person, or that plant, or that animal, or even that star in a galaxy, to come into existence. Natural selection plays no part in the evolution of a single human being. We do not include in the mechanism of growth the possible adversities which did not befall it and hence did not prevent it. The same principle of development holds for the evolution of a single human being; nothing is gained in understanding this evolution by considering the adverse chances which might have prevented it.

In our search for a reasonable cosmic view, we turn in the first place to common understanding. Science largely relies for its subject matter on a common knowledge of things. Concepts of life and death, plant and animal, health and sickness, youth and age, mind and body, machine and technical processes, and other innumerable and equally important things are commonly known. All these concepts apply to complex entities, whose reality is called into question by a theory of knowledge which claims that the entire universe should ultimately be represented in all its aspects by the physical laws governing the inanimate substrate of nature. "Technological inevitability" has alienated our relationship with nature, with work, with other human beings, with ourselves. Judgment, decision, and freedom of choice, in other words *knowledge* which contains a moral imperative, cannot be ordered in the form that some technological scientists believe. For there is no mechanical ordering, no exhaustive set of permutations or combinations that can perform the task. The power which man has achieved through technology has been transformed into spiritual and moral impotence. Without the insight into the nature of *being*, more important than *doing*, the soul of man is imperilled. And those self-transcendent ends that ultimately confer dignity, meaning and identity on man and his life constitute the only final values worth pursuing. The pollution of consciousness is the result of mere technological efficiency. In addition, the authors in this Series recognize that the computer in itself can process information—not meaning. Thus we see on the stage of life no moral actors, only anonymous events.

Our new theory of knowledge, as the authors in this Series try to demonstrate, rejects this claim and restores our respect for the immense range of common knowledge acquired by our experience of convergence. Starting from here, we sketch out our cosmic perspective by exploring the wider implications of the fact that all knowledge is acquired and possessed by relationship, coalescence, convergence.

We identify a person's physiognomy by depending on our awareness of features that we are unable to specify, and this amounts to a convergence in the features of a person for the purpose of comprehending their joint meaning. We are also able to read in the features and behavior of a person the presence of moods, the gleam of intelligence, the response to animals or a sunset or a fugue by Bach, the signs of sanity, human responsibility, and experience. At a lower level, we comprehend by a similar mechanism the body of a person and understand the functions of the physiological mechanism. We know that even physical theories constitute in this way the processes of inanimate nature. Such are the various levels of knowledge acquired and possessed by the experience of convergence.

The authors in this Series grasp the truth that these levels form a hierarchy of comprehensive entities. Inorganic matter is comprehended by physical laws; the mechanism of physiology is built on these laws and enlists them in its service. Then, the intelligent behavior of a person relies on the healthy functions of the body and, finally, moral responsibility relies on the faculties of intelligence directing moral acts.

We realize how the operations of machines, and of mechanisms in general, rely on the laws of physics but cannot be explained, or accounted for, by these laws. In a hierarchic sequence of comprehensive levels, each higher level is related to the levels below it in the same way as the operations of a machine are related to the particulars, obeying the laws of physics. We cannot explain the operations of an upper level in terms of the particulars on which its operations rely. Each higher level of integration represents, in this sense, a higher level of existence, not completely accountable by the levels below it yet including these lower levels implicitly.

In a hierarchic sequence of comprehensive levels each higher level is known to us by relying on our awareness of the particulars on the level below it. We are conscious of each level by internalizing its particulars and mentally performing the integration that constitutes it. This is how all experience, as well as all knowledge, is based on convergence, and this is how the consecutive stages of convergence form a continuous transition from the understanding of the inorganic, the inanimate, to the comprehension of man's moral responsibility and participation in the totality, the organismic whole, of all reality. The sciences of the subject-object relationship thus pass imperceptibly into the metascience of the convergence of the subject and object interrelationship, mutually altering each other. From the minimum of convergence, exercised in a physical observation, we move without a break to the maximum of convergence, which is a total commitment.

"The last of life, for which the first was made, is yet to come." Thus, Convergence has summoned the world's most concerned thinkers to rediscover the experience of *feeling*, as well as of thought. The convergence of all forms of reality presides over the possible fulfillment of self-awareness—not the isolated, alienated self, but rather the participation in the life process with other lives and other forms of life. Convergence is a cosmic force and may possess liberating powers allowing man to become what he is, capable of freedom, justice, love. Thus man experiences the meaning of grace.

A further aim of this Series is not, nor could it be, to disparage science. The authors themselves are adequate witness to this fact. Actually, in viewing the role of science, one arrives at a much more modest judgment of its function in our whole body of knowledge. Original knowledge was probably not acquired by us in the active sense; most of it must have been given to us in the same mysterious way we received our consciousness. As to content and usefulness, scientific knowledge is an infinitesimal fraction of natural knowledge. Nevertheless, it is knowledge whose structure is endowed with beauty because its abstractions satisfy our urge for specific knowledge much more fully than does natural knowledge, and we are justly proud of scientific knowledge because we can call it our own creation. It teaches us clear thinking, and the extent to which clear thinking helps us to order our sensations is a marvel which fills the mind with ever new and increasing admiration and awe. Science now begins to include the realm of human values, lest even the memory of what it means to be human be forgotten. In fact, it may well be that science has reached the limits of the knowable and may now be required to recognize its inability to penetrate into the caprice and the mystery of the soul of the atom.

Organization and energy are always with us, wherever we look, on all levels. At the level of the atom organization becomes indistinguishable from form, from order, from whatever the forces are that held the spinning groups of ultimate particles together in their apparent solidity. And now that we are at the atomic level, we find that modern physics has recognized that these ultimate particles are primarily electrical charges, and that mass is therefore a manifestation of energy. This has often been misinterpreted by idealists as meaning that matter has somehow been magicked away as if by a conjuror's wand. But nothing could be more untrue. It is impossible to transform matter into spirit just by making it thin. Bishop Berkeley's views admit of no refutation but carry no conviction nevertheless. However, something has happened to matter. It was only separated from form because it seemed too simple. Now we realize that, and this is a evolutionary change; we cannot separate them. We are now summoned to cease speaking of Form and Matter and begin to consider the convergence of Organization and Energy. For the largest molecule we know and the smallest living particles we know overlap. Such a cooperation, even though far down at the molecular level, cannot but remind us of the voluntary cooperation of individual human beings in maintaining patterns of society at levels of organization far higher. The tasks of Energy and Organization in the making of the universe and ourselves are far from ended.

No individual destiny can be separated from the destiny of the universe. Alfred North Whitehead has stated that every event, every step or process in the universe, involves both effects from past situations and the anticipation of future potentialities. Basic for this doctrine is the assumption that the course of the universe results from a multiple and never-ending complex of steps developing out of one another. Thus, in spite of all evidence to the contrary, we conclude that there is a continuing and permanent energy of that which is not only man but all life. For not an atom stirs in matter, organic and inorganic, that does not have its cunning duplicate in mind. And faith in the convergence of life with all its multiple manifestations creates its own verification.

We are concerned in this Series with the unitary structure of all nature. At the beginning, as we see in Hesiod's *Theogony* and in the Book of Genesis, there was a primal unity, a state of fusion in which, later, all elements become separated but then merge again.

However, out of this unity there emerge, through separation, parts of opposite elements. These opposites intersect or reunite, in meteoric phenomena or in individual living things. Yet, in spite of the immense diversity of creation, a profound underlying convergence exists in all nature. And the principle of the conservation of energy simply signifies that there is a *something* that remains constant. Whatever fresh notions of the world may be given us by future experiments, we are certain beforehand that something remains unchanged which we may call *energy*. We now do not say that the law of nature springs from the invariability of God, but with that curious mixture of arrogance and humility which scientists have learned to put in place of theological terminology, we say instead that the law of conservation is the physical expression of the elements by which nature makes itself understood by us.

The universe is our home. There is no other univers than the universe of all life including the mind of man, the merging of life with life. Our consciousness is evolving, the primordial principle of the unfolding of that which is implied or contained in all matter and spirit. We ask: Will the central mystery of the cosmos, as well as man's awareness of and participation in it, be unveiled, although forever receding, asymptotically? Shall we perhaps be able to see all things, great and small, glittering with new light and reborn meaning, ancient but now again relevant in an iconic image which is related to our own time and experience?

The cosmic significance of his panorama is revealed when we consider it as the stages of an evolution that has achieved the rise of man and his consciousness. This is the new plateau on which we now stand. It may seem obvious that the succession of changes, sustained through a thousand million years, which have transformed microscopic specks of protoplasm into the human race, has brought forth, in so doing, a higher and altogether novel kind of being capable of compassion, wonder, beauty and truth, although each form is as precious, as sacred, as the other. The interdependence of everything with everything else in the totality of being includes a participation of nature in history and demands a participation of the universe.

The future brings us nothing, gives us nothing; it is we who in order to build it have to give it everything, our very life. But to be able to give, one has to possess; and we possess no other life, no living sap, than the treasures stored up from the past and digested, assimilated, and created afresh by us. Like all human activities, the law of growth, of evolution, of convergence draws its vigor from a tradition which does not die.

At this point, however, we must remember that the law of growth, of evolution, has both a creative and a tragic nature. This we recognize as a degenerative process, as devolution. Whether it is the growth of a human soul or the growth of a living cell or of the universe, we are confronted not only with fulfillment but with sacrifice, with increase and decrease, with enrichment and diminution. Choice and decision are necessary for growth and each choice, each decision, excludes certain potentialities, certain potential realities. But since these unactualized realities are part of us, they possess a right and command of their own. They must avenge themselves for their exclusion from existence. They may perish and with them all the potential powers of their existence, their creativity. Or they may not perish but remain unquickened within us, repressed, lurking, ominous, swift to invade in some disguised form our life process, not as a dynamic, creative, converging power, but as a necrotic, pathological force. If the diminishing and the predatory processes co-mingle, atrophy and even death in every category of life ensue. But if we possess the maturity and the wisdom to accept the necessity of choice, of decision, or order and hierarchy, the inalienable right of freedom and autonomy, then, in spite of its tragedy, its exclusiveness, the law of growth endows us with greatness and a new moral dimension.

Convergence is committed to the search for the deeper meanings of science, philosophy, law, morality, history, technology, in fact all the disciplines in a trans-disciplinary frame of reference. This Series aims to expose the error in that form of science which creates an unreconcilable dichotomy between the observer and the participant, thereby destroying the uniqueness of each discipline by neutralizing it. For in the end we would know everything but *understand nothing*, not being motivated by concern for any question. This Series further aims to examine relentlessly the ultimate premises on which work in the respective fields of knowledge rests and to break through from these into the universal principles which are the very basis of all specialist information. More concretely, there are issues which wait to be examined in relation to, for example, the philosophical and moral meanings of the models of modern physics, the question of the purely physico-chemical processes versus the postulate of the irreducibility of life in biology. For there is a basic correlation of elements in nature, of which man is a part, which cannot be separated, which compose each other, which converge, and alter each other mutually.

Certain mysteries are now known to us; the mystery, in part, of the universe and the mystery of the mind have been in a sense revealed out of the heart of darkness. Mind and matter, mind and brain, have converged; space, time, and motion are reconciled; man, consciousness, and the universe are reunited since the atom in a star is the same as the atom in man. We are homeward bound because we have accepted our convergence with the Cosmos. We have reconciled observer and participant. For at last we know that time and space are modes by which we think, but not conditions in which we live and have our being. Religion and science meld; reason and feeling merge in mutual respect for each other, nourishing each other, deepening, quickening, and enriching our experiences of the life process. We have heeded the haunting voice in the Whirlwind.

The Möbius Strip

The symbol found on the cover of each volume in Convergence is the visual image of *convergence*—the subject of this Series. It is a mathematical mystery deriving its name from Augustus Möbius, a German mathematician who lived from 1790 to 1868. The topological problem still remains unsolved mathematically.

The Möbius Strip has only one continuous surface, in constrast to a cylindrical strip, which has two surfaces—the inside and the outside. An examination will reveal that the Strip, having one continuous edge, produces *one* ring, twice the circumference of the original Strip with one half of a twist in it, which eventually *converges with itself*.

Since the middle of the last century, mathematicians have increasingly refused to accept a "solution" to a mathematical problem as "obviously true," for the "solution" often then becomes the problem. For example, it is certainly obvious that every piece of paper has two sides in the sense that an insect crawling on one side could not reach the other side without passing around an edge or boring a hole through the paper. Obvious—but false!

The Möbius Strip, in fact, presents only one monodimensional, continuous ring having no inside, no outside, no beginning, no end. Converging with itself it symbolizes the structural kinship, the intimate relationship between subject and object, matter and energy, demonstrating the error of any attempt to bifurcate the observer and participant, the universe and man, into two or more systems of reality. All, all is unity.

I am indebted to Fay Zetlin, Artist-in-Resident at Old Dominion University in Virginia, who sensed the principle of convergence, of emergent transcendence, in the analogue of the Möbius Strip. This symbol may be said to crystallize my own continuing and expanding explorations into the unitary structure of all reality. Fay Zetlin's drawing of the Möbius Strip constitutes the visual image of this effort to emphasize the experience of convergence.

R.N.A.

Preface

This is no "scientific" inquiry in the conventional sense of the term: it lacks the customary scholarly apparatus. There are hardly any footnotes, and only a few references to supporting or dissenting opinion. There is a list of readings attached at the end of the book, but it is meant as a recommendation for further study rather than as evidence of sources I have used. Nor has it been possible to compile a meaningful index; a detailed Contents has been put in its place. In a word, the reader will have to do without some of the standard crutches of comprehension. He or she is expected to draw on his or her intellectual capital, experience, and common sense.

I am dealing with an issue with which I wrestled 50 years ago when, before World War II, I published a pamphlet entitled *The Price of Liberty*. I regret that for obvious reasons I cannot use this title again for the present essay. It expresses my concern more precisely than any title I can think of, including the one I have chosen. It takes for granted that liberty or freedom, terms I shall use synonymously, is generally acknowledged as a value of the highest order, at least in the West. But when we ask under what conditions freedom can be established and maintained, a serious and even paradoxical problem arises. As I showed then, and as we shall discover again, *freedom is safe only so long as it is associated with certain constraints*. This, however, seems to be a price that Western man is no longer willing to pay.

The reasons for this refusal are manifold. They ultimately reflect the fact that we find ourselves in the midst of a revolutionary transformation of global magnitude. In order to lay the ground for a new viable order, vast institutional reforms will be required. But if freedom is to prevail, no less important will be a change in the basic attitudes of all social strata in the realms of political, economic, and cultural relations. Such a change goes against a tradition of long standing, a tradition that is deeply rooted in private and public conduct throughout the West. So we must ask, What are the chances for achieving a new order, both stable and free?

As I have tried to find an answer, my thinking has undergone a significant transformation. My earliest ruminations go back to the battles of El Alamein and Stalingrad, when the ultimate victory of the Allies was assured and the time seemed ripe for reflecting on the postwar world. I confess that at the time I shared the optimism of Winston Churchill, who expected the three leading powers—the United States, Britain, and the Soviet Union—to form a triumvirate that would establish lasting peace and welfare all over the globe.

Subsequent drafts mirrored my growing doubts about this or any optimistic vision. They reflected the successive shocks that befell the postwar era: the atomic explosion with its ever more ominous aftermath, the Cold War, the McCarthy interlude, our awakening to ecological dangers, the microelectronic revolution with the threat of long-term mass unemployment. Each one of those shocks was, and some still are, a potential, if not already an actual, menace to both stability and freedom.

And yet I have not mentioned what may well become the worst threat: world terrorism. For all the other dangers mentioned, there are, at least in principle, remedial responses, though we may lack the wisdom to apply them. But is there an effective answer to persistent political, not to speak of purely criminal, terrorism other than a police state?

This is not the only limitation of my inquiry. I had to bring it to a conclusion while the process of transformation was in full swing. Its further course may raise problems that cannot be foreseen today. This is all the more likely because I am concerned only with the first steps toward a new viable order, and with a minimum program of reform designed to that end. But for at least pondering those problems the time is overdue.

Acknowledgments

At the head of the list of those to whom my thanks go out, stands Robert L. Heilbroner, to whom this essay is dedicated. If the strains of a ten-year struggle with a highly intricate topic have not left more traces on the text, this is due to his extraordinary skill as an expositor and his relentless demand for clarification. But his contribution far exceeds literary cosmetics. Being himself deeply concerned with the problem I am discussing, he was my first, and very likely will remain the most severe critic I am going to encounter. Perhaps the greatest service he has rendered me has been his unwavering conviction that what I attempted to do could be done. Though he by no means agrees with all my conclusions, I see in him a coauthor of this book.

My very special acknowledgment is due to Dr. Ruth Nanda Anshen, who has founded, plans, and edits the Convergence Series, a section of Praeger Special Studies, in which this book appears. A close friend for many years, it was she who introduced me to the scholarly audience of this country, by including an earlier publication of mine in World Perspectives, another internationally renowned series issued under her editorship. As in the past, her wise counsel, her steady but patient encouragement have been a constant stimulation.

Next I mention Stanford Pulrang, a collaborator of old standing. As in the past, he checked the consistency of my arguments against the overall frame of reference I have chosen. Again he played the role of the Devil's advocate to perfection.

For many helpful suggestions in detail, but also for a critical evaluation of my exposition as a whole, I owe sincere thanks to Murray Brown, Professor of Economics at the University of Buffalo. I feel the same obligation toward some of my German friends and colleagues. Their list is headed by Marion Gräfin Dönhoff. Once a star student of mine, she is now a publicist, and Chief Editor of the *Zeit*, the most prominent weekly in the Federal Republic of Germany. The list also includes Harald Hagemann and Heinz Kurz, both Professors of Economics at the University of Bremen, and Claus Dieter Krohn, Professor of History at Lüneburg University.

A special word of thanks is due to Frau Irmtraud Brummerloh, Department Secretary at the University of Bremen. With extraordinary skills she prepared a difficult manuscript, composed in what to her is a foreign language. For the accommodating manner in which the printing process itself was handled, I am deeply obliged to the staff of Praeger Publishers.

Again it is my privilege to express my sincere appreciation to the Lucius Littauer Foundation for awarding me a grant to cover the expenses connected with the technical completion of the manuscript.

I must not conclude these acknowledgments without giving visible expression of the profound gratitude I feel toward Hanna and Dr. Ernest Lustig, my younger daughter and my son-in-law. They served as experimentees for me to check whether what I was committing to paper was palatable also to the nonspecialists, and they helped me greatly during the various stages of proofreading. But their essential contribution lies elsewhere. In a spirit of loving care, they have provided the physical and the human environment in which I have been able to continue my scholarly work.

HAS FREEDOM
A FUTURE?

1   An Era in Travail

Few intellectual ventures are as risky as the attempt to locate the place of one's own time on the evolutionary scale of history. Scant information, conflicting experiences, hope, and fear are bound to blur understanding and to mislead judgment, as the record of historical prophecies shows only too clearly. Still, on rare occasions there is one indicator that can serve as a signpost—when the present is widely taken as a radical break with the past. It is my contention that the second half of the twentieth century gives evidence of just such a break.

It does not follow from this that we can foretell with confidence the trend of events. But we may be able to conjecture in what manner any conceivable trend is likely to differ from what went before. To be more precise, we cannot say whether the decades ahead will raise civilization to a higher level or lay it open to progressing disintegration, not to speak of nuclear destruction. But today this very ignorance reveals more than the trivial fact that in some way the future is always unknowable. Ours is a *new kind of ignorance* that is the consequence of the changes that are occurring.

Those changes consist in the weakening, if not elimination of major constraints that shaped the political, socioeconomic, and cultural development since the dawn of history. Let me mention only the power of tradition transmitted through the family and through political and ecclesiastic authority, the pressures of the natural and social environments, manifested in scarcity of resources, or the hierarchies of sex, race, caste, and class.

In the past those contraints were taken as ineluctable by those experiencing them, thus rendering the future less of an enigma because at least some of its properties could be foreseen by simply extrapolating from present experience. From now on, however, *the future will have to be more and more the result of our deliberate choices* at every level of human activity. Though we still cannot predict the actual course of events, we can gauge *possible alternatives* as the result of particular actions or, what may be even more fateful, of specific omissions.

GLOBAL TRANSFORMATION AND ITS CONFLICTING TRENDS

These alternatives and, especially, their repercussions on freedom are the main topic of this essay. At this introductory stage I want to offer no more than a brief outline of the major issues we are going to encounter. But before doing so, I must give some proof that a transformation of the asserted scope is indeed in progress. This is best done by listing some of the cataclysmic changes that mark our era—changes whose origin reaches back to World War I and even beyond, but that have gained their full momentum only since the end of World War II.

There is, first of all, the rise of socialist systems in several variants, embracing by now more than one-third of the world's population. Not only are these systems a challenge to the power and even the viability of capitalist democracy, the sociopolitical order of the West, but they have already forced upon it far-reaching modifications, exemplified by the formation of the welfare state. There is, second, the reawakening of the Asiatic civilizations, of Islam as a political force, and the end of colonialism. Third, we are moving toward the political and social equalization of the nonwhite races and of all the other strata of the hitherto "subject population," not least among them women and youth. Fourth, a worldwide takeoff into economic development and, at least in the mature regions, the potential conquest of poverty are under way.

Next are the release of atomic energy, the push into space, and the new technology symbolized by the computer, climaxing in what is hailed as a microelectronic revolution in factories and offices. Nor should we pass over the breaking of the genetic code and a rapidly expanding genetic technology.

At another level lie the subtler but no less momentous transformations in the realm of the mind: new technologies of communication; the opening up of the unconscious and its symbolic expression in forms of art; a philosophy and even a theology centering on human existence and the sanctity of immanent experience. Underlying many of these changes is the most "subversive" force of all: the spread of knowledge among ever wider strata in all societies, advanced and primitive, exposing to critical thought what hitherto had been accepted as absolute truth or as inscrutable fact.

At first sight we seem to be confronted by a medley of occurrences whose coincidence might be pure chance. But once we break through surface appearances, all those changes reveal themselves as manifestations of one and the same underlying impulse—to cast off fetters of the past forged by a harsh nature, by even harsher human masters, and by the harshest despot of all: ignorance.

Still, it may be one and the same impulse that is at work, but it is met with diametrically opposed evaluations. To some, especially to many scientists, this breaking of fetters seems to open the way to a new Jerusalem or, to use Friedrich Engels' phrase, to mark the "end of pre-history." To them an old dream narrated in fairy tales and utopias, ancient and modern, is turning into reality—man finally is master of his fate in global association with his fellow men.

However, there are many others to whom this headlong rush into new knowledge and revolutionary action is about to tear asunder the ties that have held human communities together since the dawn of history. To them the prospect is one of self-destruction in atomic wars, ecological catastrophes, and, the ultimate penalty inflicted on such a Promethean rebellion, the madness of universal anarchy.

Contradictory as these visions are, they point to some of those alternative futures with which we are concerned. At the least they bring to light the open-endedness of the present hour or, if you wish, its "dialectics," alluding to opposite effects of one and the same cause. Take as evidence the simultaneous prospect of mass welfare and mass incineration opened by some of the new technologies; a wider scope for self-government but also the rise of new tyrannies made possible by the political upheavals; the conflict between worldwide industrialization and climatic disaster; the chances of a race healthier in body and mind but facing grave threats to personal integrity implied in the biopsychological innovations.

Thus, when judged from the point of view of preserving and advancing civilization, this breaking of old fetters gives rise to a destructive as well as a constructive potential. But by the same token we can conclude that, to the extent to which the constructive potential materializes and the destructive tendencies can be averted, mankind will indeed move to a new stage in the time-honored process of *emancipation*, with the promise of a higher level of material welfare, of more equitable interrelations, and of a wider range of freedom.

EMANCIPATION AND FREEDOM

Underlying this inquiry is the axiom that emancipation, conceived as the realization of the constructive potential in the revolutionary changes of our era, is the common goal in all contemporary societies, West, East, and South. Where they differ, and what in particular divides the so-called Free World from its totalitarian opponents, is the function assigned in this process to the free initiative of individuals and groups. No doubt, Western emphasis on such initiative is much older than the process of emancipation itself. Greek and Roman influences merged with the Judeo-Christian tradition not only in raising the free individual to the rank of an absolute value but also in making the individual the major instrument of mundane progress. There we touch on the cardinal problem of this essay: Can we take it for granted that realization of the emancipatory potential of our age and, even more, the efforts required to ward off simultaneous destructive tendencies, will maintain or even strengthen the role of the free individual?

At first sight such a doubt seems to contradict what we described as the driving force of emancipation, the casting off of the fetters of the past. Is this not by its very nature an act of liberation? Before we can answer this question, we must state more explicitly what we mean by freedom or liberty.

In trying to do so, we are forewarned by Isaiah Berlin that there are "more than two hundred senses in which this protean word has

been recorded by historians of ideas." Fortunately, in relating freedom to emancipation we greatly simplify our task. Freedom reveals
itself then as the condition in which the thinking and acting of
individuals and groups are not limited by external but removable
constraints, always excepting irremovable barriers such as the laws
of nature or man's biopsychological constitution. In the briefest
formulation, freedom is the *power of self-determination* over the range
open to human decision making. It can be specified as follows:

1. To the extent to which no external force reduces our command over at
    least some segment of our life space, we enjoy *private freedom*.

2. To the extent to which we codetermine with the other members of our
    group the range of private freedom and also the constraints that affect
    other segments of our life space, we enjoy *public freedom or self-govern-
    ment*.

In this definition the distinguishing mark of "freedom-limiting"
constraints is their *externality*. From this it follows that we do not
regard self-constraint as such a limitation. Rather, we accept it as
a particular type of self-determination. However, when we try to
state in positive terms what external constraints consist of, we find
ourselves entangled in a controversy that today radically divides
political theorists and also the agents of political practice.

The controversy centers on the relationship of the welfare state
to freedom. In name both sides fight under the same banner of
freedom, but closer examination reveals that they fly quite different
flags. The opponents of the welfare state see an illegitimate constraint of freedom in any *deliberate interference* with the social process and, in particular, in interference on the part of governments—what we henceforth shall call public controls. In other words,
to them the maximum range of freedom is assured so long as public
controls are absent or at least reduced to the minimum indispensable to maintain "law and order."

However, it can easily be shown that this circumscription of illegitimate constraints is much too narrow. This is implied in Ana-
tole France's well-known taunt that both the rich and the poor are
free to sleep under bridges. His jibe points to a type of constraint
that is quite different from, but no less stringent than, any public
control. Obviously freedom understood as self-determination can

exist only where everyone has access to the means on which the attainment of his or her chief ends depends. Such access is greatly reduced in a class structure with large inequalities of income and wealth, or in a regime where racial or sexual discrimination prevails.

But such blocks are not laws of nature. They are in principle removable, and thus *legitimate targets of public control*. It is a major aim of the welfare state to do away with such impersonal constraints, and we can specify *egalitarian freedom* as the major goal of emancipation.

PLANNING AS AN INSTRUMENT OF STABILIZATION

It follows that the success of emancipation depends on a distinct relationship between individual and society. This may not be obvious so long as we dwell on the initial phase of emancipation, the breaking of past constraints. But for emancipation to succeed, a second phase must follow in which new but *enduring relations are established between man and nature and other men*—relations that can integrate themselves into a new order of society. Our stress on duration is not meant to exclude what cannot be excluded—evolution beyond the present stage of emancipation. What it is intended to exclude is "permanent revolution" as a social process.

What, then, we must ask, are the forces that make the transition possible from the disorder of the initial phase of emancipation to a new order of enduring relations? To find the answer, it will prove helpful to have another look at the constraints of the past. So far we have interpreted them as no more than shackles on freedom. And it remains true that those fetters created the triple bondage of economic scarcity, political domination, and intellectual and spiritual dogmatism. But those repressive features must not blind us to another aspect that might be called their *protective function*. We readily understand this if we think of some of the destructive forces that threaten us today: the constant menace of atomic war, the pollution of the environment, the erosion of behavioral norms. In contrast, those past constraints safeguarded over long stretches of history the integrity of the natural and sociopolitical order, though they may themselves have been the outgrowth of ignorance, superstition, and primitive taboos. At any rate they were a protection against the greatest danger of our own age, the self-destruction of mankind.

Against this background we begin to understand what it means when we say that the first phase of the stage of emancipation, through which we are passing today, sweeps away not only the repressive constraints of the past but also its protective curbs. Moreover, it stands to reason that the destructive potential thus released cannot be automatically neutralized by the forces that create it. Indeed, there is no alternative to placing the protection of the emancipatory process in the precarious *custody of our own hands*.

Of course, we must not overstate our case. There are domains where human intervention will always be limited: the laws of nature will in all likelihood remain our masters for good. But in view of the open-endedness of the evolution to which we are exposed, the constructive potential of emancipation will gain the upper hand only if the ambivalent forces of the past are replaced by a deliberate, unidirectional pursuit of the emancipatory path.

We define such pursuit as public *planning*, a term under which we subsume the elaboration of programs of reform but also their application with the help of specific public measures. In applying the term "planning" to the measures I have in mind, I may of course expose myself to a basic misunderstanding. As used today in popular discussion, the term conjures up all the mistakes and social outrages of totalitarian regimes. On the other hand, in its brevity the term is a convenient expression to cover a wide range of stabilizing policies that lack any authoritarian flavor, such as monetary and fiscal controls, social security, or an incomes policy to prevent inflation.

When understood in this sense, planning has two functions. Without impairing the prevailing sociopolitical system it modifies its operation, a *macro aspect*. But to be effective it must also influence the behavior of the individuals and subgroups that compose the system, in such a manner that they can integrate themselves into orderly macro states and processes—the *micro aspect* of planning.

However, will not effective planning, in building up a new orderly macro state, by its very effectiveness reduce freedom? Even if it is true that public controls can remove inegalitarian constraints (as was shown earlier) so that planning can serve as a medium of expanding freedom, is this not perhaps an exception?

BEHAVIORAL CONFORMITY AS A CONDITION FOR STABILITY

To find the answer, we must first of all examine more closely the nature of what we defined as "micro forces" and as "macro structure," and their interrelationship. There can hardly be any doubt about what we mean by a micro level of human activity and by the entities encountered at that level. They are objects of immediate experience, and there cannot be any question whether they are "real."

This is not so obvious when we speak of a macro level and of entities such as groups, societies, or nations. Are we simply using a terminological shortcut in pointing to an aggregate of individuals, or are we speaking of supraindividual bodies with properties and interests different from those which attach to their constituent individuals?

This is a problem that has puzzled philosophers since ancient times, a problem that has acquired special significance in the present ideological dispute between West and East. The modern Western conception of such collective phenomena is rooted in the ideas of the Enlightenment. Most of its representatives regarded the notion of, say, society as a mere fiction, the underlying reality being the individuals who compose the collectivity in question, with no other than individual interests at stake.

In sharp contrast with this conception, some conservative thinkers, and especially the modern totalitarians, have reified such collective entities as suprapersons. The salient point was stated in Mussolini's Charter of Labor, which proclaimed: "The Italian nation is an organism having ends, life, and means of action superior to those of the separate individuals and groups that compose it." The case is different in original Marxism, in which a socialist order was understood as a "free association of producers." It is all too clear in contemporary social bodies that wear the label of socialism.

In a way we meet here on the political plane a revival of the metaphysical and epistemological dispute that medieval "realists" and "nominalists" carried on about the nature of "universals," that is, of generic concepts pertaining to classes of objects. In formal terms the question at issue was indeed the same as the one we are debating today in political science: whether a generic term like "society" refers to a real entity or is merely a name for a multitude of particulars.

Here an important clue can be found in a peculiar solution offered to that Scholastic dispute by Pierre Abélard, popularly known in a rather different context. While denying that universals have an existence separate from the particulars, he nevertheless insisted that they augment our knowledge of reality. They do so by pointing to what is "similar" or even "identical" in a multitude of particulars. The universal is, so to speak, located *in* the particular as that which relates it to other particulars.

Obviously this viewpoint is relevant for our concerns. It gives an interpretation to sociopolitical macro notions that establishes them as legitimate concepts in their own right. Though what they describe are not independent entities with a life of their own, under certain conditions such collectivities are more than the mere sum of individuals assembled on some territory or engaged in some activity. Without losing their singularity as persons, those individuals form a *distinct structure* whenever they display a particular common trait—in Abélard's terminology, when they *conform* in their basic outlook, a conformity that manifests itself in mutually compatible behavior patterns. It is such conformity that distinguishes a community from a crowd by creating the stability and durability of what we understand as macro states and macro processes.

EXTERNAL ROOTS OF CONFORMITY: ACCULTURATION AND PLANNING

Still, we must not overstress the analogy. To the Scholastic mind, conformity among the elements of a generic concept was an intrinsic quality—thus was the world created. However, conformity of behavior patterns is not given once and for all. It must be accomplished by a process of *acculturation* and be reproduced in every generation. This is a process by which the average individual is committed to certain epistemological and ethical criteria. In Geoffrey Vickers' formulation, in order to form a viable group, its members must "share some assumptions about the world they live in, and also some standards by which they judge their own and each other's action in that world." It is such a commitment that conciliates their personal strivings with the requirements of macro order.

There is, it is true, a doctrine that implicitly denies the need for acculturation. It is the doctrine of anarchism, which postulates that man is inherently social, that is, instinctively attuned to the requirements of group stability—in some ways resembling such social creatures as ants and bees. That which has made behavior patterns discordant and has generated destabilizing conflicts, the doctrine continues, is the stinginess of nature and the inegalitarian order of society. However, these obstacles to harmony can be removed. Once they are removed, the unconstrained strivings of individuals will prove fully compatible with one another, establishing a stable collectivity.

Those preconditions have, of course, never materialized in other than quite primitive societies, so that no evidence can be adduced for this optimistic prognosis. History and daily experience present us with a more complex image of *Homo sapiens*. He is not fully autonomous and self-contained, as some philosophers of the Enlightenment saw him. Nor is his mental outlook entirely the product of social relations, a view popular among Marxists, though hardly shared by Marx himself. To the unbiased observer, man appears as a *hybrid of individuation and socialization*—the former a constituent of his biopsychological makeup, the latter the product of acculturation.

The combination of those basic elements has varied greatly in the course of history and, in the prevailing view, the preponderance of individuation is seen as a major advance in civilization, especially when judged by the criterion of personal freedom. All the more is it important to stress the perpetual significance of socialization, and of acculturation as its medium. But we must also be aware of the large variety of modes through which acculturation, and thus conformity, can be achieved. We can distinguish at least four such modes: the subtle, pervasive influence of the family, including at primitive levels a more comprehensive kinship system; stimuli issuing from the reigning culture, operating as formal and informal education; political and ecclesiastic authority; and the impersonal pressures of natural and social mechanisms.

At the present stage of emancipation, planning is to serve as a substitute for the traditional modes of acculturation in a world in which impersonal pressures have weakened and cultural stimuli have turned ambiguous under the impact of rival styles of life—even the family is ceasing to fulfill its traditional function. At the same time the danger is real that the planners, when they misconceive their substitute function, may invade the sanctum of personal freedom, enforcing conformity in disregard of the legitimate claims of individuation.

This is reason enough for us to ask whether a certain degree of conformity is really as indispensable for personal existence as his metabolism is with nature. Suppose we lose ourselves completely in the concerns of the moment, not caring for the morrow—a supposition that, with the spreading desire for instant gratification, is more than a theoretical speculation. In this frame of mind we might indeed dispense with all constraints, if we are willing to pay the price. Unfortunately the price is no less than our survival and, if such "Bohemianism" were to become the dominant style of life, the survival of civilization.

In our discussion of egalitarian freedom we have already indicated why this is so. For freedom to persist, man must persist—a condition that depends on the persistence of a macro order. But no macro order can persist unless it is sustained by the behavior of its micro units. In a word, *specific constraints on our conduct are a prerequisite of enduring freedom.*

SPONTANEOUS CONFORMITY

But need such constraints be imposed by external forces such as planning? Can they not be engendered by self-restraint on the part of the micro units—an attitude we explicitly excluded from the list of freedom-limiting factors? Here we now encounter an issue that, in various modifications, has played a significant role in social history, and that must be a major concern to anyone interested in a satisfactory balance of freedom and order.

Of course, one may wonder whether the very ability to constrain oneself is not a product of acculturation, and thus of an external factor. Even so, once the ability exists, applying it is a spontaneous act, especially when it springs from a recognition of the stability-promoting effect of the ensuing conformity. We deal, then, with *spontaneous conformity* as the prime source of individual behavior patterns—no doubt the ideal combination of individual self-determination and macro order.

Still, in this ideal form spontaneous conformity presupposes a degree of rational understanding of social processes that, even in smaller and less complex societies than industrial capitalism, far exceeds the ability of ordinary people. So it is not surprising that in practice spontaneous conformity has usually been associated with a particular mode of external pressure.

What is at stake was formulated more than 2000 years ago when Thucydides, through the mouth of Pericles, praised the Athenians for their obedience to those "unwritten laws transgression of which provokes reprobation by general sentiment." What he had in mind was the power of public opinion, a *societal constraint* that takes the form of approval or disapproval of an individual's behavior on the part of the group to which he or she belongs. No doubt an external constraint, this force yet differs from the limitations imposed by most of the modes of acculturation previously mentioned, not to speak of enforcement through planning. Neither is it backed by physical coercion, the *ultima ratio* of all political controls, nor does it resemble impersonal mechanisms. Rather, such societal constraints remind one of the stimuli that issue from the cultural environment and might even be identified with them. What is decisive is the fact that, *though the stimulus is external, the response is spontaneous*, springing from the realm of individuation. This is certainly so whenever the stimulus is rejected. But even conforming to it can be interpreted as a spontaneous act, especially if the constraint is "internalized," thus creating a feeling of self-determination after all.

NONCONFORMITY AS A SOURCE OF EMANCIPATORY PROGRESS

I have been dwelling on societal influences on spontaneous conformity because they define the minimum constraints of freedom compatible with macro order, and at the same time the maximum constraints compatible with autonomous individuation. And yet, when stated in this summary manner, our conclusion is open to a serious misunderstanding. One might infer from it that conformity, and especially spontaneous conformity, is always beneficial to both freedom and order, whereas nonconformity must be rejected once and for all as detrimental.

My mere affirmation of emancipation contradicts such an inference. After all, we are concerned with the elaboration of institutional and attitudinal *changes* in the interest of consummating the emancipatory potential of our time. This is equivalent to saying that the criteria for visualizing the world and of acting in it, which ruled in the past, have to a large extent lost validity and need to be replaced by new criteria. The rightful claim for some degree of nonconformity goes even further. Even in periods in which the life-style of a society is more or less settled, the thinking and acting of its members must not be totally conformist if at least a modicum of freedom is to be preserved.

From this we can only conclude that the emancipatory goal must not be conceived as a macro order from which all frictions are removed. *Some degree of disorder is the price of autonomous individuation, and thus of genuine emancipation.* For this reason we shall henceforth plead for what we shall call quasi order and quasi stability, admitting some degree of disorder and instability, so long as the critical threshold, below which the persistence of society is in danger, has not been overstepped.

It seems idle to speculate about an "optimum proportion" in which individual autonomy and conformity should combine. The balance of freedom and order has greatly differed in the course of history. Those historical combinations appear to have been influenced not only by geography, geology, and technology, but also by different ideas about the human type most esteemed. However, one should not conclude from this that the *feasible* relations between autonomy and conformity are totally indeterminate. Certainly the two extremes on the spectrum—unlimited autonomy and total conformity—are clearly self-destructive. The former is incompatible with any macro order, and thus with individual survival; the latter reduces man to a subhuman level—a warning to any overzealous planner.

TRANSITION TO A HIGHER STAGE OF EMANCIPATION

What we have so far discussed is the tolerable and even desirable impact of nonconformity on a settled pluralistic society. A much wider range of nonconformity characterizes the *transition* from one stage of emancipation to the next. There, what I should like to label "positive" nonconformity has a creative function: to discover and to apply new epistemological and ethical criteria. What this amounts to can best be understood if we depict such a process of transformation in a simple model.

We start out from the more or less steady movements at the macro level of a society with a settled life-style, sustained by the quasi conformity of its micro units. At a given moment a change occurs in the behavior of some micro units—the type of change illustrated earlier in the list of transformations that characterize our century. A good example from the past is the victory of the abolitionists in the United States. But the model is valid also for earlier emancipatory transformations, such as the actualization of the Encyclopedist ideas in the French Revolution.

In either case the nonconformist thrust—the attack on slavery or on absolutism—met with the resistance of the conformist strata, and at the initial stage it could not be predicted who would win out in the end. It took a civil war or a major revolution to decide the issue. But once the nonconformist forces had triumphed, novel criteria—embodied in Article XIII of the U.S. Constitution and in ordinances of successive French constitutions—became the principles of a new conformity. In both instances the process extended over many decades, but was never reversed.

One might be tempted to draw a parallel with the accepted model of biological evolution, with its mutants at the micro level of the organism that is exposed to natural selection through the competition of various mutants and through the pressure of the environment. But a certain formal similarity must not obscure the differences between biological and social evolution. Whereas the successive steps in nature are the result of blind forces, in society they are mediated by purposeful decisions of the micro elements. And though the violence that has frequently accompanied social mutation gives the impression that, as in nature, the breakup of the original equilibrium is a sudden, discontinuous event, closer examination reveals in almost every instance that the new forces had gradually ripened in the womb of the old, decaying order.

But what complicates social evolution far beyond the vicissitudes to which biological evolution is exposed is that this ripening into a new quasi equilibrium is by no means a straightforward process. The nonconformist agents of transformation, though aware of the failing validity of the inherited criteria, hardly ever have at the outset a clear notion of how the abstract concepts of their new criteria are to be translated into institutional practice. Not only the means suitable to attain the desired end, but the concrete *gestalt* of the end itself, is indistinct. Moreover, they have to contend not only with those who cling to the past but also with the indifference of those who are totally absorbed by their private concerns, not to speak of competitors who pursue utopian schemes representing a counterculture.

Applying all this to the phase of transition through which we are passing today, we witness the disintegration of the late Victorian quasi equilibrium. This compels the champions of the new stage of emancipation to do battle not only with those who strive to return to the old style but also with all sorts of "negative" nonconformists who say "no" to what was and is, and do not even sense what is to be.

It is not the first time that Western civilization has been exposed to such a commotion. At least twice before—at the end of the Middle Ages and, as just indicated, during the transition from absolutism to liberalism—the Continental centers passed through interims of disintegration. From our point of view, it is significant that the first victims were earlier carriers of freedom. In both instances transformation was achieved by autocratic regimes. A contemporary example is, of course, the Soviet Union, whose transition to a "free association of producers" has by now lasted more than two generations without the end being in sight.

The outstanding exception until recently was England, with an unbroken tradition that reached back to the late Middle Ages. More than any other Western society, its history demonstrates the strategic role that micro forces play in the conciliation of freedom and order, as well as the limits of such harmony under the conditions of late capitalism.

Considering those contradictory tendencies and the strength of countervailing forces, one might well conclude that the outlook for egalitarian freedom sustaining and being sustained by a quasi-stable order is dim. But what makes it so are ultimately not objective hindrances, but the overall subjective response to the challenge of our era. In all leading nations of the West, governments as well as the majority of the people, judging by their voting record, dodge the issue by attempting a retreat to the political and socioeconomic style of the nineteenth century, that is, to an earlier stage of emancipation. But if it is true that the former stabilizers are rapidly withering away, such a flight into the past can only accelerate social and cultural disintegration. No less disheartening is the shallow optimism, if not indifference, displayed by the majority of social scientists.

For all these reasons my primary objective in writing this essay is not to gain acceptance of the answers I am going to offer to the specific problems that confront us, but to provoke a serious debate about the questions I am raising. Let us remember that, as nature abhors a vacuum, so does society not long tolerate gross instability and the anomie that is its cause as well as its effect. Those who wield power have a weapon of last resort: autocracy.

Emancipation in Historical Perspective

If our introductory survey has demonstrated anything, it is the fact that ideas such as emancipation, freedom, or equality cannot be properly discussed in an ahistorical vacuum. They acquire precision only in a specific cultural context and are for that reason history-bound. Therefore, if we are to comprehend where we are today, we should know something about where we came from. In particular, we must find out what freedom, equality, and, not least, social stability meant at various stages of emancipation. This is the program for this and the next chapter.

THE TAKEOFF INTO EMANCIPATION

Our first task is to locate and to date the events that mark the takeoff into emancipation. This is no easy undertaking, because the major factors that have promoted this development entered history at quite different stages. Reviewing the list of recent dramatic changes, we can reduce them to three strategic determinants: socio-political liberation, intellectual enlightenment, and technological progress. Actually, their impact on civilization made itself felt in reverse order. Rudimentary technology with advances in farming, husbandry, and craftsmanship, establishing some mastery over nature, reaches back into prehistory. Enlightenment or critical thinking, on the other hand, belongs to a much later period. Its origin can be traced to ancient China, Egypt, and Mesopotamia, reaching full bloom in Greek philosophy and science.

The difficulties of dating multiply when we turn to sociopolitical liberation. At first sight one might relate its beginnings to events such as Hammurabi's legislation 4,000 years ago, followed by the Mosaic law, Solon's reforms, the Roman Twelve Tables, and canon law. Indeed, each of these measures attempted to lighten the bondage of some subjugated stratum. But in contrast with the acts of emancipation that pervade the modern age, all those reforms bear one telltale characteristic: They were essentially concessions from above, alleviations of duties rather than assertions of rights. Rare were the endeavors of the subjugated populations to seize the initiative—such as the slave revolt led by Spartacus—and, like that revolt, they all miscarried.

The names of Wycliffe and Huss symbolize a radical change. It began in the later fourteenth century, marking the end of the European Middle Ages. What started as an ecclesiastic dispute assumed political form in the rebellions of the Lollards in Britain and the peasantry in Bohemia, demanding basic social reforms. Though both movements were suppressed, the revolutionary impulse lingered on, to break out with even greater violence in the Peasants' War of the sixteenth century. The new spirit, transforming the earlier pleas for alleviation into a struggle for emancipation, resounds in the famous rallying cry:

> When Adam delved and Eve span
> Who was then the Gentleman?

The slogan is telling because it reveals the mixture of religious and material motives in the minds of the rebels, pressing the traditional dogma into the service of overthrowing dominion. Thus a taboo was rejected that no Amos or Gracchus had questioned: the legitimacy of the prevailing sociopolitical order.

From then on, release from dominion turned into liberation by the liberated. And such liberation began to combine with technological and intellectual-spiritual progress. It is this unified advance of all strategic forces to which our notion of emancipation refers.

ABSOLUTISM AS THE FIRST EMANCIPATORY STAGE

We shall now survey the major stages of this process. In accordance with what we earlier said of the 'dialectics" of this process, of the concurrence of promise and threat and of the twofold nature of the prevailing constraints—repressive as well as protective—our story will reveal many conflicting tendencies.

It begins with the rise of the *absolute state*, an event that coincides with the Renaissance in art and science, and the Reformation in the Christian Church. In opening new vistas of knowledge, in laying the ground for a new technology, and, on the other hand, in proclaiming the spiritual equality of all Christians, Renaissance and Reformation were indisputable forces of emancipation.

This is not so obvious in regard to the new political organization manifested in the centralized power of national states. In contrast with the relatively mild controls of the medieval order, about which more will be said presently, some of the absolute monarchs introduced a nearly totalitarian rule, including not only central regulation of production and consumption but also the religion of the subjects. So at first, as far as mastery of man over man is concerned, absolutism appears as a step backward on the path of emancipation. This impression is strengthened when we remember that subsequent emancipatory breakthroughs in the English, American, and French revolutions had as their target absolutist abuses.

In order to recognize that, in spite of those retrograde features, absolutism was ultimately a progressive force, we must look at the political order—or, rather, disorder—that preceded it. In doing so, we take our bearings from the more distant era of the early Middle Ages and the then dominant regimes. Their political organization is well illustrated in the doctrine of the "two swords," a strange combination of collective controls with separation of the controlling powers.

Civil governments and their delegates were supposed to be in charge of all worldly affairs, including the preservation of peace and the administration of justice, whereas all spiritual concerns were in the keeping of the Church. However, and this is a salient point, the head of the Church had an edge over the secular rulers. Being invested with the ultimate authority in matters of faith and morals, he could, in cases of dispute, excommunicate his worldly opponent and thus deprive him of the fealty of his subjects.

It seems fair to say that for some centuries this doctrine reflected tolerably well the actual balance of double-headed dominion—a balance that constrained the behavior of civil governments in their relations with one another and with their subjects. This is true not only of the higher ranks of the feudal hierarchy, on whose loyalty the power of the secular rulers largely rested, but also of the dealings of the feudal lords with persons and groups of lower rank. Even the serfs, though tied to the land, were not helpless tools in the hands of their masters. They could claim their protection, a claim that was sustained by the ecclesiastical authorities.

So, too, the medieval towns enjoyed a large degree of political independence, coupled with a successful kind of self-government. Considering further the evolution of feudal parliaments and of Church councils, one can discover rudiments of self-government even on the national and ecumenical scale. Ultimately the universally shared hope of salvation and fear of damnation imposed some voluntary discipline on the pursuit of worldly interests.

It would be a misapplication of terms were we to describe those relationships as media of freedom or self-determination, as we have defined those terms. Still, the presence of rival authorities in an age of greatly limited communication created a margin of autonomy at every level of the feudal hierarchy. Moreover, at least in dealing with fellow Christians, personal and public behavior was never totally dissociated from acknowledging a modicum of spiritual equality, and thus of responsibility toward neighbor and subject.

In stressing these protective constraints, we are not trying to idealize the medieval order. Not only did practice deviate more often than not in the direction of repression, but from the twelfth century on, the delicate balance of forces was undermined by the destructive rivalry of the secular and the ecclesiastical powers, the imperial claims of pope and emperor. What originally had the semblance of an international society was torn asunder into a medley of national states, each claiming absolute sovereignty in secular and spiritual matters. Domestically, especially on the European continent, the hierarchy of feudalism gave way to a ruthless competition of the various estates—high and low nobility, clergy, and urban units—for predominance in national affairs. Therefore the rise of absolute monarchies must be understood also as a response to the threat of anarchy and as a safeguard of national unity.

As we know only too well, the forces released in the nations that absolutism created at a later stage degenerated into destructive nationalism. But at the outset they were emancipatory in a peculiar sense. By depriving the feudal lords of their political privileges and subjecting the cities to the sovereignty of the state, the first inroads were made into the status order and the dependencies of the past. The complex hierarchy of the medieval society was transformed into a conglomerate of individual subjects—a development from which the future *citizen* sprang. At the same time *entrepreneurial attitudes* were fostered in contrast with the homeostatic conduct of the past.

Far from being an attitude innate in all men at all times, as the classical economists were later to proclaim, the new economic outlook had to be nursed by governmental stimuli, best shown by the regime of Colbert in France. Also symptomatic is a remark by Frederick the Great of Prussia, when he wrote on one of his rescripts: "The plebs"—his term for the rising bourgeoisie—"will never give up the humdrum tune, unless you drag them by their noses and ears to their profits."

What we find in those stimuli are acts of "liberation from above," not unlike the paternalistic forms of liberation that occurred during the premodern era. But they eventuated in the violent self-assertion on the part of the ruled in the revolutions of the seventeenth and eighteenth centuries. In view of what was to follow, another aspect of those transformations is equally important. From the outset both the citizen and the entrepreneur—the prototypes of emancipation under absolutism—bore *individualistic* traits that reached full bloom during the liberal era.

Thus the political and economic institutions and the intellectual climate of industrial capitalism were an outgrowth of the absolutist age. But only when associated with a *new technology* did emancipation create what we call today the middle classes. To grasp the full significance of this all-pervasive factor, we must avoid a narrow interpretation of technology as merely material, that is, as physical, chemical, and biological engineering. Of equal importance were the political and socioeconomic inventions of the postmedieval era, in part recapturing institutions of the ancient city-states—a standing army, a secular civil service, new methods of public finance, the rationalization of law, progressive monetization of economic trans-actions—culminating in the working rules of *representative govern-ment* and of a *free market*. Still, it was indeed the machine technol-ogy of the first industrial revolution that, side by side with the concurrent political revolutions, had the strongest impact through a progressive elevation of the standard of living.

LIBERALISM AS THE SECOND STAGE

With the substitution of some form of constitutional government for the divine right of kings, and with the introduction of industrial technology into the individualistic framework of market relations, the *second stage of emancipation* was reached: the era of *liberalism*. It lasted until the outbreak of World War II, and in retrospect ap-pears to many as a golden age when compared with our own terror-stricken century.

The spread of representative and progressively democratic gov-ernments, and the apparently limitless opportunities for enterprise and wealth creation, set the Western nations on a path that prom-ised steady extension of personal independence and material wel-fare. The rate of progress differed widely from nation to nation and from class to class. But the conviction prevailed that what mat-tered for individual contentment and social stability was the contin-ual upward movement of the social pyramid as a whole rather than the distance that separated the base from the apex. And there is no doubt that, all over the West, political power was diffused into rudiments of self-government, and that in the long run some of the fruits of technological progress fell to every stratum of the popula-tion. Therefore it is hardly surprising that, toward the end of the nineteenth century, capitalist democracy was accepted as the legit-imate framework of social relations and as the warranted tool for their further improvement—a steadily growing socialist opposition notwithstanding.

In the eyes of the major beneficiaries—the upper classes—this development was traced back to the breaking of the political and economic fetters of the past. They were convinced that the predic-tion of Adam Smith in the previous century had come true: a "sys-

tem of natural liberty" was replacing the earlier regimes of constraint, assuring not only a maximum of personal freedom but also
the stability and progress of society at large in a peaceful comity of
nations. But when we confront this liberal ideology with historical
reality, we shall discover that this simplistic explanation rested on
a profound misinterpretation of the actual forces at work.

As is well known, the *ideological principles* on the basis of which
the new stage of emancipation was interpreted by its contemporaries, grew out of a secularized version of the medieval natural-law
doctrine, with emphasis on the natural rights of individuals as the
foundation on which every society rests. Society obtained its legit-
imation through the fiction of a social contract voluntarily entered
into by free men pursuing their personal interests. The pre-modern
maxim of mutual responsibility, even if imperfectly applied in
practice, was explicitly relegated to benign neglect.

Those ideological principles found their first political embodiment in the U.S. Declaration of Independence: government with
the consent of the governed, equality, and the right to liberty under the law. With certain variations they found their way into all
liberal constitutions on the European continent. Moreover, similar
"natural" principles were read into economic relations: individual
freedom in market transactions and equality of bargaining partners
when exchanging "equivalent values," both maxims safeguarded by
free competition in the commodity and labor markets.

We have long since learned to see through the harmonist pre-
tense of those ideas, considering the manner in which they took
shape in the course of the nineteenth century. We need only to
remember the subversion of the "consent" of the governed by a
strictly limited franchise, or the striking inequality of the bargaining partners in capitalist labor markets. But when moving from
theory to practice, we meet with a true paradox: the perversion of
the ideology served as a stabilizing constraint.

POLITICAL AND ECONOMIC LIBERALISM

Speaking first of the *political* realm, it was far from obvious that
regimes deprived of the "organic" bonds of feudalism, and also of
the bureaucratic "clamp" of absolutism, could achieve and maintain
stability. But, far from surrendering their destiny to a truly egali-

tarian order, in all Western nations the upper strata of society retained political power, giving their policies, foreign no less than
domestic, a conservative bent. By limiting expansionist tendencies
to colonialism, they established a new balance of power, supported
domestically by gradual reforms that appeased the disfavored strata
and defeated new revolutionary upheavals. In these policies no less
than in interpersonal relations, relics of the religious and moral climate of the past established and preserved a homogeneous culture.
Every Western nation adopted its own brand of Victorianism and,
at least on the surface, of practical restraint.

Ideology and reality stand in a more complex relationship when
we examine the *economic* sphere. There we encounter the *locus* where
the nonindividualistic tradition was first subverted and a peculiar
form of freedom was introduced. In this process an important role
fell to the new science of economics, whose major purpose was to
demonstrate that order in the market could arise from the unconstrained behavior of the bargaining partners. The solution to the
riddle was found in the competitive struggle of independent private
enterprises, each striving for maximum pecuniary gain.

Pursuit of pecuniary gain appeared to the classical economists to
be the epitome of freedom, because no external control regulated
such individual behavior. From this fact they drew the conclusion
that the profit motive was a universal propensity inherent in human
nature, a crude metaphysics that was easily challenged by psychologists and anthropologists. Moreover, we indicated above the tute-
lage to which the absolutist bureaucracy subjected the rising middle classes in order to wean them away from a homeostatic tradition.
Still, it is more than doubtful whether such an "educational" policy
would have been universally successful, had it not been supported
by more powerful forces: *impersonal pressures* arising from the natural, social, and technological environment of early capitalism.

There are few if any historical periods on record in which all
environmental forces combined to a comparable degree in molding
economic behavior. The dominant ones were mass poverty and
personal isolation in a competitively organized class structure characterized by the appropriation of the means of production by a
small minority. The outcome was a cultural climate in which economic success became the prime source of private power and pres-
tige.

Of course, we need only to think of mass poverty to realize that some of those factors had operated long before the rise of capitalism. Nor did all of them bear with equal strength on all strata of society. The pressure of penury on the agrarian population reaches far back into the Middle Ages and beyond. As far as urban life is concerned, large-scale flight from the land, and later labor-saving technology, created conditions in the labor markets that, far into the nineteenth century, pushed wages down to the minimum for survival. In fact, the industrial worker was exposed to the triple coercion of subsistence wage, of employment insecurity, and of the mechanical control of working time through the factory system. One certainly must not forget that the transformation of the serf into the free laborer was a big step toward emancipation. But during the early decades of industrialism, the freedom to sell one's services to the highest bidder was eclipsed by the need to do so.

Material privation was, of course, no problem for the upper strata of capitalist society. There the pecuniary motivation was engendered by the pressure of competition—a peaceful struggle, but still a struggle for survival. To this was added the psychological pull of wealth creation, originally regarded in the Puritan tradition as a sign of divine election, but more and more secularized as a source of worldly power and self-esteem. As Werner Sombart stated it, in the premodern era power created wealth; in the modern era wealth created power.

Thus, without speculations about perennial human propensities, a realistic evaluation of the environment in which capitalist marketers went about their business fully explains their transformation into "economic men" displaying a uniform behavior pattern easily predictable by their partners in the market and evoking compatible responses. But even such conformity assured stable provision only so long as buyers and sellers were sufficiently mobile to be able to respond promptly to changes in demand and supply. For labor such mobility was achieved through the abolition of guild regulations. For the entrepreneurs it was the prevalence during the early industrial era of small and medium-sized business units coupled with the absence of large stocks of fixed capital, a technological condition that permitted speedy transfer of resources to the most profitable fields.

Though the ensuing benefits were heavily weighted in favor of capitalists, one could with some justification speak of a "market mechanism" that, in the absence of any planning authority, created order out of the spontaneous actions of countless buyers and sellers. The mechanism at work can best be described as a negative feedback process through which deviations from stability were eliminated by obverse movements, a mechanism formulated in the law of supply and demand.

Still, this process of impersonal stabilization proved rather precarious, as the further course of capitalist development made only too clear. Technical progress moving in the direction of a steadily rising scale of business organization, and monopolies springing up on both sides of the social fence, more and more reduced the mobility of the system and its capacity for rapid adjustment. Large periodic fluctuations—business cycles—took the place of the theoretically predicted "moving equilibrium" of output and employment.

This trend might well have destroyed the viability of an uncontrolled market order then and there, had not other impersonal factors opened a safety valve. These were rising aggregate demand in steadily expanding markets, owing to the increase in domestic population, and the constant creation of new outlets for exports and highly profitable investment opportunities in what would one day be called the Third World.

HOW TO ASSESS THE LIBERAL ERA

In summing up, we ask, How are we to evaluate this second stage of emancipation under the aspect of freedom and stability? The answer is complex because we must distinguish between the viewpoint of its contemporaries and our own, observing as we do from the distance of a later stage of emancipation.

To the contemporaries of the liberal era—certainly of its apex in the latter part of the nineteenth century—it appeared as a reign of freedom, the like of which had never been achieved in past history. Indeed, constraints exercised by men and man-made institutions were narrowed down to a minimum. An ever expanding corpus of human rights protected the private freedom of every person—an inner sanctum the boundaries of which no outside agent, however powerful, might legitimately transgress. In a similar manner, at least in western Europe and the United States, civil rights ensured public freedom, the codetermination of the remaining public controls by the controlled themselves. Finally, absence of outside interference with economic transactions fostered the belief of actors and observers that "private" enterprise was the same as "free" enterprise.

No doubt a feeling of almost unlimited autonomy prevailed in the broadening ranks of the beneficiaries of the liberal regimes. And even the majority of the still underprivileged believed that liberal institutions offered the best opportunity for the betterment of their lot. We know today that behavior in the private, above all in the economic, realm by no means emanated from sovereign choices of self-determining individuals, as the ruling ideology proclaimed. Religious and moral traditions carried over from premodern times and formalized in more or less rigid conventions, together with the various pressures of the environment, molded the attitudes of the average person—constraints hardly less tight than the fetters of the past.

However, to arrive at such a verdict one must have passed on to the next stage of emancipation, where critical thought dissolved much of tradition, and where new material and social technologies weakened, if not obliterated, the impersonal constraints. Contrariwise, to the contemporaries the ruling conventions and the environmental pressures appeared *immutable*, almost of the order of the laws of nature, an analogy often drawn with the laws of the market. Seen in this light, those constraints did not affect individual self-determination, and one can understand that at least the beneficiaries of liberalism believed that they enjoyed the widest range of freedom ever attainable.

A word must be added about the standards on which the "selves" of this era oriented their behavior. We have seen that individualism reigned supreme not only ideologically but certainly in economic practice. And one can admit that for the goal of wealth accumulation in a market system, ruthless pursuit of self-interest was a suitable means. Of course this could be so only because what we today call infrastructure was organized and maintained by public policy.

Under the protection of this remnant of absolutism, individualism assumed even a moral guise. Memories of a different evaluation still echoed in the early stages of capitalism, when in the eighteenth century Bernard de Mandeville, in his *Fable of the Bees*, spoke of "private vices" creating public benefits. But with the extension of market transactions, emphasis shifted to the benefits that pecuniary striving was to reap. In the end the pursuit of private gains became glorified as a virtue—vide the writings of Benjamin Franklin or the Horatio Alger novels. Thus, when Marx wrote that under capitalism ceaseless accumulation of profits is "Moses and the prophets," he aptly chose a religious symbol.

Much of what has been noted so far can be entered on the credit side of the liberal ledger. But, as we have already indicated, its Achilles heel was instability, a consequence of the growing rigidity of the market structure and of unequal distribution of incomes. But a still deeper threat to both the political and the economic balance arose in the sphere of *international relations*.

To grasp this, one must turn from the nations of the West to the nonwhite majority of mankind. Many of those peoples carried on a primitive life-style formed under the pressures of nature and tradition, or had become the object of colonial exploitation. This is not to deny that a network of global economic relations had developed, and it was customary before 1914 to speak of a "natural division of labor" among the regions of the world. However, events would soon show that the prevailing status was no more than a passing phase. One-sixth of mankind owning the globe's workshops, exchanging part of their output on highly favorable terms with the rest of the world, deriving additional profits from the lending of their surplus wealth, and on that basis claiming political and cultural leadership—clearly this was anything but a "natural" global order. It was the product of very special circumstances and one-sided power relations that had grown from an advance of the West in science and technology, as well as in political and business organization—but an advance of hardly more than 300 years. There was nothing in this progress that was bound to its place of origin. Rather, the vehement force of this expansion bore the seed of a violent reaction.

One might have expected that the socialist opposition in the West would press for a more egalitarian world order. However, not only did this opposition lack political power, but with few exceptions its leaders shared the pro-Western bias of their class enemies. This is not difficult to understand once we realize that the economic and social advance of Western Labor was bound up with the success of industrial expansion. In the face of protestations of international solidarity of working-class interests, the urge to defend a privileged position welded all classes into communities of interest: an aggressive nationalism. On such precarious foundations rested the balance of the Western world—the balance of a spinning top.

3   The Present Stage of Emancipation

The spinning top tumbled over in 1914, setting in motion a chain of events the rush of which has not abated to this day. When Sir Edward Grey, the British foreign secretary during those fateful days, spoke the prophetic words "The lamps are going out all over Europe, we shall not see them lit again in our lifetime," he was more perceptive than the statesmen in the other belligerent nations. But even he could not have realized the full gravity of his words, for the simple reason that is was no "law of history," but deeds and omissions of actors who might well have chosen another course, that turned a falling rock into the mightiest avalanche of modern history.

GENERAL CHARACTERISTICS

World War I started as a contest among old-fashioned nationalisms. There was no iron logic in the fact that no compromise peace emerged from the military stalemate of 1916. Nor was it an inexorable destiny that turned the Russian Revolution of early 1917 into a totalitarian government rather than into a constitutional regime. Such speculations are more than futile hindsights; they open our eyes to missed opportunities by highlighting the role of the human factor, then as now.

This is far from asserting that anything is possible at any time. Unresolved problems of the past and the domestic or international tensions thus built up always mark off tendencies that neither human wisdom nor human folly can divert. Looked at from the turn of the century, these tendencies clearly pointed in the direction of a further stage of emancipation: politically in the unstable regimes of imperial Germany and even more so of czarist Russia; socioeconomically in the precarious class structure all over the West; internationally in the uneasy relationship of the European powers with their colonial dependencies, with the ancient civilizations of the East, and even with the United States.

An unbiased observer could have perceived clear indications of these trends while the arms were still silent. Statistics of world production would have revealed the approaching economic hegemony of the United States. The Russian revolution of 1905, even if abortive, could not but demonstrate the shakiness of the regime. Reading Tocqueville might have revealed that, once it had developed its potentialities, Russia might well become a counterpart of U.S. dominance. Japan had already proven the military and economic prowess of a nonwhite nation. On the other hand, British policy in India revealed the self-destructive tendencies of an imperialism that was willing to foster indigenous industries. And even China, for millennia the bastion of traditionalism, had taken the first steps toward emancipation.

Implied in what we are saying is the belief that it was the *bouleversement* of a *thirty years'* war rather than a gradual evolution that turned this third stage of emancipation into a century of derangement of practically all civilizations, both advanced and primitive. This makes it difficult to sort out the long-term emancipatory trend from accidents bound up with the sudden and all-encompassing torrent through which it is struggling.

In speaking of a thirty years' war I assume that the two world wars and the uneasy truce between 1919 and 1939 form a continuum. It is true that during the interwar period none of the major nations faced one another on the battlefield. But never before were so many civil wars fought in the brief span of two decades: Russian, Italian, German, Spanish, and the Kuomintang phase of the Chinese revolution. Nor can it be denied that some roots of World War II must be sought in the settlements of World War I, and in the intervening revolutions that themselves were in a large measure responses to those settlements.

Thus, what might have taken generations in a peaceful development was compressed into a few decades, during which the map of three continents was redrawn and an alternative to capitalist democracy took shape. Within the capitalist orbit even the leading European powers were reduced to second-rate status, the political, military, and economic predominance having shifted to the New World. White colonialism came to an end without making the globe a more peaceful place. Capitalist and collectivist regimes have been polarized, as have the "have much" and the "have little." The absence of hot war among the big powers since 1945 may in the end reveal itself as no more than another armistice.

No less radical have been the transformations *within* the nations of the West and in the so-called Third World, not to speak of the "Second World" of collectivism. In the first group, mass democracy has become a political reality through the enfranchisement of the entire adult population. The welfare state has replaced liberal capitalism, and Victorian manners and morals are being cast off. In the Second and Third Worlds, tribal and semifeudal rule or foreign domination have given way to more or less dictatorial regimes, and in many of those regions population growth has outrun, and thus annulled, economic development. In sum, internationally and intranationally more fetters have been broken during this century than in the preceding millennia. But the ultimate goal of emancipation—a new political, socioeconomic, and cultural equilibrium—has so far eluded us.

THE INTERNATIONAL SCENE

We shall now examine more closely what we earlier called the dialectics of the present stage of emancipation, that is, the conjoined promises and threats related to this development. We do so in order subsequently to gauge the institutional and attitudinal changes required to shift the balance toward the promises, and also to discover the impact of those changes on the scope of freedom.

Beginning with the *international* scene, we find ourselves in an area in which the negative features predominate. At the same time we must admit that what happened during this century has only aggravated a situation with which the more peaceful liberal age failed to cope: the contradiction between the claim of the national state to absolute sovereignty and the demand for stability in international relations. The rudimentary growth of a "law of nations" since the seventeenth century has been a poor substitute for the medieval principle of a Christian community, however often transgressed against. The new law of nations was little more than the acceptance of certain rules of chivalry in the handling of military conflicts. The decision of a government to enter into such a conflict was reserved to its own *raisons d' état*. What for a while still maintained a modicum of international conformity among the dominant states was little more than royal intermarriages, mercenary armies capable of changing allegiance at short notice, and the supremacy of French culture during the early centuries of the modern era.

The final breakup of anything resembling an international order and the rise of militant nationalism resulted from two movements, both carrying the banner of emancipation: the struggle for national liberation and the domestic victory of the middle classes, symbolized in the dates of 1776 and 1789. The disruptive effect of those movements remained latent during much of the nineteenth century. Britain's rise to international supremacy and an all-Western boom of industrialization gave life to a new balance of powers. Still, the Franco-Prussian War of 1870 was an indication that no voluntary balance was stable enough to adjust the "European Concert" to changes in the relative strength of its members. Finally, the events of the twentieth century, beginning with the Russo-Japanese War, made it clear that neither ententes nor peace pacts nor the mirage of a League of Nations could guard against imperialist ambitions. And even the setting up of the United Nations has left the balance of atomic terror as the only effective balance.

The decision to start an international conflagration has always rested with the great powers. But the powder kegs to feed such an explosion were often provided by the nationalist aspirations of smaller nations. One may argue that both the Ottoman and the Habsburg empires had long forfeited a positive role in international affairs, yet one must admit that the "balkanization" of eastern Europe that resulted in their dissolution contributed in great measure to the outbreak of both world wars. At the time of this writing the danger zone has moved to the nationalist stirrings in the Near East, Africa, Southeast Asia, and Central America.

Decolonization is another example of recent emancipation that so far has resulted in destabilization. Even when affirming it as an essential step toward worldwide political equalization, we must not overlook the fact that the colonial regimes had provided an integrating force where tribal and regional antagonisms formerly had wasted vast human and material resources. Nor is there any denying that some members of the now ruling strata exhibit the worst features of their former masters.

Thus, in the absence of effective constraints, both institutional and spiritual, the victories of the third stage of emancipation have left international relations in a state of latent anarchy. The proclamation of "one world" was never more than a chimera, as had been 100 years earlier the hope that free trade might establish world economic unity and universal peace among the thus interdependent nations. Some political romantics even dreamed of imperialist expansion as an integrating force—a utopia that was confounded not only by decolonization but also by the rise of Communist nations as new aspirants for world domination. The decline of the European powers has added to instability. It replaced a competitive balance, however unstable, with the bilateral monopoly of the United States and the Soviet Union (and China as a future third contender).

With some nostalgia one remembers a critical moment during the negotiations preceding the setting up of the United Nations. As mentioned earlier, at that time a triumvirate of the United States, Britain, and the Soviet Union was envisaged, in Churchill's words, as the instrument for "building up the permanent structure of peace throughout the world." Though paying lip service to the "sovereign equality of all peace-loving states," the Big Three considered an initial trusteeship over the rest of the world. This vision of course rested on the assumption that they themselves remained united—already an illusion in 1943 when they discussed joint world control. Since then, with a prelude during World War I, the spirit of the Crusades has lurked behind the pious declarations of summit meetings, based on the belief in the demonic nature of the opponent, whose annihilation is seen by many on either side as the discharge of a sacred mission.

THE DOMESTIC SCENE

Turning now to the *domestic* scene, we shall examine the emancipatory upheavals mainly under the aspect of their effect on the

West as the locus of responsible action. Once more we must begin by stressing the immense scope—political, socioeconomic, and cultural—and the unprecedented speed of the transformation. It is a process that easily fits into the life span of any person born around the turn of the century. Not a few such persons have prospered beyond expectation. But one can only marvel at the endurance and adaptability of those many millions who have mastered loss of status and possessions, occupational demotion, or transfer in mass or individual migration, not to mention the horrors of outright persecution. Perhaps the "malaise" about which social and clinical psychologists complain today has its roots in a rate of change that greatly overtaxes mental and even nervous capacity.

A similar discrepancy between the speed of change and the capacity for adaptation afflicts the *institutions* that the liberal era has bequeathed to us. In every Western country the entire adult population—with a generous interpretation of adulthood—has acquired equal voting rights, so that political democracy in the most comprehensive sense is now the dominant constitutional principle.

And yet we see its operation endangered by populist rebellions and, in some countries, by growing apathy. This hardly betrays a preference for autocratic regimes on the part of the newly enfranchised masses. It seems that, rather than strengthening the operation of democratic institutions, universal participation in the political process hampers it. One major reason is that this universality, irrespective of sex and past standards of maturity, has broken a basic agreement on values that characterized the minority democracies of the past. It was such agreement that permitted small and slow mutations in the sociopolitical structure through trial and error and the gradual education of the electorate.

Compare with this procedure the continuous tug-of-war between the executive and the legislative powers that rages today in the citadels of representative government. It also reflects the new time scale of change in the need for quick decisions on major matters of foreign and domestic policy, on which opinions are sharply divided and the full import of which is beyond the grasp of routine thinking.

Frustration of the governmental apparatus in dealing with social instability threatens the legitimacy of the democratic system, that is, the belief that the prevailing institutions are the most appropriate for contemporary society. As a consequence a skeptical passivity is spreading over ever broader groups of the potential electorate in some countries, leaving the outcome of elections to the vote of fluctuating minorities. Only two generations ago a nation could be aroused to go to war in order to make the whole world safe for democracy. Who in the West believes today that this is a feasible goal and one worth dying for?

Failure to adjust the constitutional process to a mass democracy endangers political stability. By way of contrast, it is the very *success* of organized capitalism that jeopardizes economic stability. It was largely impersonal pressures—mass poverty, unbridled competition, and a Puritan work ethic, together with vast opportunities for market expansion—that maintained a precarious balance during the liberal era. Today's predicaments have arisen from the fact that none of these impersonal stabilizers has survived unhampered.

The quickening progress of material technology together with the democratization of the political system has freed the broad masses from the bondage of scarcity. Monopolistic organizations of both capital and labor have mitigated the competitive struggle, promoting economic security, as do the income and employment policies of the welfare state. Lured by growing affluence, more and more social groups surrender the austerity of acquisitiveness to the hedonist mores of a mass-consumption society.

In contrast with a past in which the large majority had to forego any chances of a good life to eke out a bare subsistence, for the first time in history a steadily widening range of choices has fallen to the masses of the West—promoting not only freedom but also growing equality of living standards and of social status.

However, when judged by the requisites of a functioning market, those gains are offset by a dangerous loss. The weakening of the former barriers to economic freedom is removing an essential stabilizer of the past: the uniform behavior patterns that had ensured the self-correcting movements of the system. Today the pattern of maximizing receipts and minimizing expenditures must contend with new homeostatic tendencies: producers striving to maintain the value of their assets or their market shares rather than maximizing profits; consumers preferring routine purchases of branded goods irrespective of price differentials. And even when profit maximization is still the dominant action directive, it has lost its former determinacy, because the time span over which profits are to be maximized is no longer fixed. In the modern organizational and technological environment, the periods of production and investment, the size of financial commitments, and the efficiency of the capital stock vary from branch to branch, from firm to firm, and even within the same firm from time to time. As a consequence, increasing or decreasing output, raising or lowering prices can each be justified as the most promising step to profit maximization according to circumstances. Thus no marketer can safely anticipate any more what the response of other marketers will be to his own action, making expectations—a strategic factor in decision making—more and more uncertain. Finally, with the self-assertion of the Third World, market expansion, one main escape mechanism of the past, meets with growing resistance.

THE RISE OF THE WELFARE STATE AND ITS PRESENT CRISIS

The overall response to these frustrations of liberal capitalism is the institutions of the *welfare state*. Not that these institutions are the result of a concerted plan of reform. As any historical review will confirm, the individual measures were taken to counteract specific exigencies, and it is only in retrospect that we can discern some systematic unity.

Beginnings can be traced far back into the liberal era, to the English factory laws and the subsequent social legislation in Germany and Britain. The strongest impetus arose from the statism that the belligerents of World War I adopted for the conduct of their economies when scarcity of manpower and material enforced central allocation and, in strategic fields, the central planning of production.

After World War I political control of the economy was generally rescinded by a return to private enterprise, except in the Soviet Union. After World War II, however, the consequences were very different, not least because of the dismal experiences during the interwar period with its catastrophic climax in the Great Depression. Some form of public control of the economy has since become the rule in all Western countries, from the near socialist regimes in

Scandinavia to the hybrid systems in Britain, on the European continent, and even in the United States. Common features of this transformation are some degree of public control of income and employment, directly through public spending and indirectly through fiscal and monetary policy, and some measure of individual security support, protecting the living standards of the victims of unequal distribution.

Such statism in peacetimea must be understood as the application of a lesson learned in the war. During those years public controls achieved what, contrary to the liberal ideology, the free market had accomplished only in brief boom periods: full utilization of the available human resources. Even without the "new economics" based on the teachings of Keynes and others, after the experience of the Great Depression the public was no longer willing to accept the cycles of boom and bust as "acts of God." They were recognized as failures of obsolete institutions.

It must also be understood that the ensuing transformations under the New Deal in America and the Beveridge reforms in Britain bore a *conservative* character in the true sense of the term. Far from intending to undermine the foundations of a capitalist order, those policies were, in Keynes' words, to serve "as the only practical means of avoiding the destruction of existing economic forms in their entirety and as a condition for the successful functioning of individual initiative." In other words, they were to provide the benefits that liberalism had in vain expected from the invisible hand guiding an uncontrolled market.

How are we to evaluate the operation of the welfare state after the passing of more than a generation? Were we commenting on this experiment, say, in the middle of the 1960s, the verdict could only be favorable. Nowhere had the violent fluctuations of the prewar era recurred. Real per capita growth doubled in the United States over what it was in pre-Depression days, not to speak of the much higher rates in Germany and Japan, where wartime destruction made it necessary to rebuild capital stocks. Everywhere the mass standard of living rose dramatically while the price level—disregarding the temporary effect of the Korean War—remained almost stable.

By greatly reducing industrial fluctuations, the "public controls," as we shall label the new policies, enhanced more than material welfare and security. By strengthening the stability of the macro processes of the economy, they widened the market chances for both business and labor, adding to the newly gained freedom of choice a novel freedom from want and risk.

Thus it is not surprising that the institutions of the welfare state were widely accepted as a new style of economic life. Even large swings in parliamentary majorities left them untouched. What only a few decades earlier was a main topic of ideological strife had become the subject of pragmatic trials. Stability, and thus permanence of controlled capitalism seemed assured.

Looking back from the vantage point of the 1980s, we must ask, What has happened to alter reality and critical appraisal so radically? The facts are incontestable: a rampant inflation, the deepest recession of the postwar era, a slow improvement hedged by new fears of inflation and apparent inability to absorb a growing bulk of structural unemployment. No wonder this has been the signal for the opponents of the welfare state—hitherto a small minority without political influence—to rally in frontal attack on the "new economics" and its public controls, the alleged causes of these grave distortions.

Thus a radical split today divides not only public opinion but also the experts in social science. The split involves real differences of views. But those differences are obscured rather than illuminated by the terms in which they are discussed. Take present-day U.S. parlance, in which "liberals" are advocates of governmental power in the service of public controls. This interpretation is in direct conflict with the history of the term, in which liberals stand for minimum intervention in the social process, a meaning that still prevails in Europe.

The term "conservative" has undergone a no less radical reinterpretation in the entire Western world. The movement that is spreading today under this label has little in common with the ideas of Burke, De Maistre, or Hegel, representative leaders of a conservative opposition during the liberal era. For them the pivotal political agents were not individuals concerned about their freedom but collective entities, in particular nations and states, with a primary interest in stability. What range of individual freedom those thinkers did acknowledge as legitimate seemed to them to be guaranteed by the "organic" structure of those suprapersonal bodies.

Apart from stressing the cultural significance of traditional morality and a religious revival, the program of contemporary conservatism has hardly any connection with that original conception. It places personal freedom first and advocates what amounts to a return to the regime of the liberal age, supported by a return to a laissez-faire economy.

In order to avoid confusion, we shall dispense with either term when discussing contemporary events. Instead we shall speak of "decontrollers" who, for the sake of maximizing freedom, aim at a minimum of government interference, whereas we shall call "planners" those who advocate public controls for the same purpose.

In siding with the planners, I want in no way to belittle the achievements of liberalism in its original meaning of decontrol, namely, extending freedom by reducing and even abolishing the power of premodern controllers: monarchs and priests, guild masters and absolutist bureaucrats. But as we have tried to demonstrate from the outset, this experience of a past era in no way offers an assurance that social decontrol and economic laissez-faire can cope with the ills that beset us today.

A SUMMARY OF THE DESTABILIZING FACTORS

The remainder of this chapter will be devoted to an exposition of those ills. It is a complex story in which economic factors play the dominant role. It may be helpful to begin with a *summary* of the major events of the postwar history of the West, and in particular of the United States.

1. At least on the surface it was *noneconomic shocks* that disrupted the balanced growth that the national economies and the world economy at large had enjoyed during the first two decades following World War II.

2. These shocks exerted their impact on the *changed structure of an organized capitalism* lacking the self-correcting feedbacks and the escape mechanisms that had bestowed on liberal capitalism a tolerable degree of long-term stability.

3. The consequence was, first, a *cumulative process of inflation*, followed by a *major recession* in output and employment.

4. The main responsibility for this course of events rests with the *planners*

who were in power during most of the inflationary phase. They failed
to apply appropriate measures for restabilization, leaving it to an administration that in principle affirmed decontrol to prevent runaway
inflation by a drastic policy of deflation.

5. This was followed by a *moderate revival*, allegedly due to a program of
   "supply-side" economics but in fact the result of the much maligned
   Keynesian arsenal of demand stimulators.

6. What this revival failed to achieve was an approximation to full employment. The major cause is a *persistent structural unemployment* due to
   a technological transformation in the mature countries and in some regions of the Third World.

7. All the more crucial has been the function of the welfare state in providing *a safety net of social security*. Without these safeguards, unemployment might well have reached the magnitude of the Great Depression
   or worse, undermining mass consumption with unpredictable sociopolitical consequences.

DEMAND INFLATION

The *first phase* of economic instability was one of *inflation*. Though
it spread over most of the globe, the time and place of origin can
be determined precisely: the change of the U.S. involvement in
Vietnam from a minor encounter to a major war. More specifically,
it was the manner in which this undertaking was financed—by bor-
rowing rather than by taxation, in a state of full resource utilization. As a consequence the increase in active money circulation,
and thus in demand, exceeded production capacity at a growing
rate, creating a typical *demand inflation*.

The reason for this course of events is not in doubt: hesitation
on the part of both administration and Congress to risk a struggle
over the distribution of a new tax burden, a struggle that might
have brought the war to a precipitate end. Conversely, to divert
the required resources from civilian to military use through a rise
in the price level—that is, a reduction of the purchasing power of
money incomes—offered two tactical advantages. The initial impact was small and, in contrast with taxation, the ensuing reduction in real income could not be traced to specific agents or parties
who might be called to account in the voting booth.

Thus the inflationary process was initiated by the combination of an expansionist foreign policy with party politics in the United States. Yet large deficits in the U.S. balance of trade owing to rising demand for war goods gradually spread inflation over the world at large. But in the United States itself the manner of financing the war was by no means the only factor at work. What goes by the name of "entitlements"—transfer payments and grants-in-aid to states and local governments by the federal government—played a growing role. There we deal with an item that the champions of the welfare state count among its major achievements, improving or at least maintaining the living standards of the poor and the elderly. And it should be remembered that during the early decades of the postwar era those payments represented a real transfer of income from one social stratum to another, remaining within the limits of fiscal orthodoxy. Only after the middle 1960s did their share in the federal budget rise from less than 25 percent to over 50 percent, and thus to more than 20 percent of the gross national product. Still, if the decontrollers denounce entitlements of the needy as the major cause of inflation, and as a shift of resources from the productive to the unproductive strata of the population, they need to be reminded that other groups, with farmers and the maritime industry as major examples, shared in those benefits. Nor must we forget the outlays for national defense, which were to a large extent a subsidy to the armament industries.

The reader may by now have missed mention of the public's favorite culprit of this circulatory distortion, the *oil cartel*. Its actions share with the Vietnam War the character of a political shock, because they were inaugurated as a weapon in the Arab-Israeli conflict. Otherwise those successive price increases were of a nature quite different from what caused a demand inflation. They reduced aggregate output, at the same time redistributing it in favor of the owners of the scarce resource. In the case of the oil monopoly the situation was aggravated by the fact that the recipients of the monopoly profits lived abroad, thus further reducing the output available for domestic consumption.

Considering its direct effects, what the oil cartel brought about was impoverishment rather than inflation. And one could expect that, with oil prices settling at some ceiling and demand inflation ceasing at the end of the war, stability would be restored, though at a higher price level and a lower level of domestically available output, redistributed at the expense of the recipients of money incomes.

In fact, a quite contrary situation developed during the 1970s when the war had ended: an inflationary trend that in the end could be reversed only by an artificially created deflation with an enormous loss of output and employment. It is in this context that the weakening of some earlier constraints and the absence of promptly applied public controls once more reveal the "dialectics" of emancipation.

COST-PUSH INFLATION

Over a considerable period demand inflation created only a slow rise in the general price level. This was mainly due to the "money illusion" of industrial Labor, who accepted today's dollar as equivalent with yesterday's. But in the course of the 1970s the conviction spread that Labor was really exposed to an insidious process of deprivation. Now a distributional struggle began that opened a new source of inflationary pressure, defined as *cost-push* inflation.

It is important to realize that nothing of this kind could have occurred while genuine competition still ruled in the labor and commodity markets. Prices were then limited by the state of demand, and business firms responded to attempts to push up money wages by curtailing output or by technological reorganization, in either case discharging some of their employees and thus creating a counterforce in the labor market. A structural change, which makes us speak of the present market structure as "organized capitalism," has largely eliminated this self-correcting mechanism. I refer to the monopolistic and oligopolistic manipulations of both market partners, supported by the social security provisions of the welfare state.

Once more we are faced with contradictory consequences of the weakening of the former constraints. Self-organization protects capital and labor from ruinous cutthroat competition. But it also permits a growing segment of industry to elude the discipline imposed by a competitive order, by enabling it to "administer" prices and wages largely irrespective of varying states of demand. Changes in commodity demand are now responded to by adjustment of output and employment rather than of prices. The ensuing fluctuations in the demand for labor do not much affect the administered level of money wages, so long as generous unemployment compensation keeps the victims of output reduction out of the labor market. What now determines prices in those "fixed-price" industries is, first of all, costs of production plus a mark-up for financing investment. Where wages may play a significant part in determining costs of production, their own level is ruled by the prices of wage goods.

The final phase of this destabilizing process was reached when the experience of a price rise transformed itself into the anticipation of a future one. The main weapon in the ensuing battle over distribution was automatic escalator clauses built into more and more wage contracts, commodity agreements, and even entitlements. But far from eliminating the negative effect of a rising price level on the real value of money receipts, and thus "helping us to live with inflation," such indexing only intensified the process of devaluation. By steadily narrowing the range of those on whom the inflationary "tax" could be levied, indexing accelerated the spiraling course and pushed the system toward hyperinflation, the total destruction of the circulatory mechanism.

The United States entered this phase in the late 1970s. It was widely regarded as a "self-exciting" process, dominated by a positive feedback of market transactions that no public policy could influence. Nothing could have been further from the truth, as the subsequent policy of deflation demonstrated only too drastically. No wage-price spiral is feasible unless it is stimulated by the tacit complicity of the monetary authorities in providing the money supply for financing higher payrolls. It was a faulty fiscal policy that started demand inflation—it was an all-too-compliant monetary policy that opened the floodgate of cost-push inflation. We shall return to this issue and ask, What prevented the guardians of the welfare state from entering the fray at a time when the costs of intervention, in terms of output and employment, would have been a trifle compared with what they proved to be when a double-digit rate of inflation had to be fought?

Last, we must assess the long-term consequences of a decade of rising inflation. There is some controversy about its effect on the *distribution of income*. Some experts maintain that, at least up to the very last phase, the relative economic status of the major strata of the U.S. population was not significantly altered. It is indeed possible that administered prices and wages enabled big business and big labor to insulate themselves from the devaluation of their receipts. The victims were then an amorphous group: small business, unorganized labor, and a medley of fixed-income recipients.

What is beyond doubt, however, is the fact that the holders of *money assets* were partially expropriated as a natural consequence of the rise in the price level, ordinary savings accounts and insurance policies being typical examples. In this way the trend toward the formation of a new oligarchy cutting across a traditional class division was intensified—the big producers facing the small-scale urban population, with farmers in the middle.

In paying so much attention to both the causes and the effects of inflation, we seem to place undue emphasis on a past stage of U.S. economic history and, for that matter, of the history of most Western countries. We do so because the future may well hold new inflationary spells in store, inflationary tendencies being inherent in the structure of organized capitalism.

THE MICROELECTRONIC REVOLUTION

Turning now to the *deflationary* phase, there is no controversy about the cardinal facts, but quite some dispute over how these facts are to be explained. Planned monetary restriction on the largest scale succeeded in bringing down the rate of price rise from a double-digit level to practically zero. But this highly desirable outcome had to be purchased by a recession that, in terms of falling output and employment, exceeded anything experienced since the Great Depression.

The Reagan administration tried to meet these unfavorable consequences with a policy allegedly based on a newfangled "supply-side" economics, which was supposed to stimulate saving and investment, thus restarting economic growth with the prospect of restoring full employment within three years. While directing their polemics against the demand-oriented, anti-recessionist weapons in the Keynesian arsenal, the measures applied by the "supply-siders"—tax reduction and public works (armaments)—were precisely those of the Keynesians. As every Keynesian would have expected, output and employment did revive—accompanied by huge and rising budget deficits, with interest rates at a record level. Also at record levels were the deficits in the balance of trade and the level of the dollar exchange rate, the latter blocking a sound development of exports.

Still, the subsequent revival, which extended to other Western regions pursuing a similar policy, shows a quite untypical and rather disquieting feature: *persistence of large-scale unemployment.* This must make us wonder whether the double-digit level of unemployment reached at the bottom of the recession was due solely to the policy of deflation and could be cured in its entirety by reflationary measures. This doubt is strengthened when we remember that, even prior to the phases of inflation and deflation, unemployment never fell below 5 percent, and that it fluctuated between 6 and 8 percent during the inflationary boom. In fact, we are confronted there with what has been labeled structural unemployment. Rather than resulting from a reduction of activity within a constant economic framework, as is true of deflationary unemployment, structural unemployment is the outcome of a lasting change of the framework itself.

Once again this change is related to an emancipatory breakthrough—this time in the realm of technology. We are referring to the so-called *microelectronic revolution*, symbolized in the computer and its rapid spread all over the globe. This is about to transform radically the modes of production and of administration within the mature regions, creating the new phenomenon of "jobless growth." But in line with the overall process of industrialization, it is also invading the Third World, thus threatening industrial production in the West.

We shall return to this issue when we study institutional changes required to safeguard the emancipatory process. Still, even at this point stressing only the negative effect of the new technological regime would misrepresent its dialectic. Not unlike earlier instances of technological innovations, the microelectronic revolution promises to liberate not only blue-, but now also white-collar workers from traditional toil and drudgery, and is to this extent an engine of liberation. Moreover, it will help in solving a problem that troubles many observers of the contemporary economic scene, the apparent fall in productivity.

And yet, if these real gains should have to be paid for by a large-scale permanent loss of working places, growing masses of workers will be transformed from recipients of market income in freely chosen jobs into state pensioners, with dark personal and political consequences. Fortunately we are still at the beginning of this transformation, and its symptoms at present show not so much in actual displacement as in the lack of absorption of newcomers by the labor market. Still, when we learn that in 1986 the rate of unemployment within the European Economic Community amounted to 12 percent, the prediction of so conservative a body as the Organization for Economic Cooperation and Development may well come true: that jobless growth and even job diminution across the entire manufacturing sector of the industrial world is the trend for the 1980s.

MALDISTRIBUTION AND ECOLOGICAL LIMITATIONS

This, however, is by no means the end of our troubles. Even jobless growth, though creating a major sociopolitical impasse, is after all growth, and thus an antidote for the other bane that has threatened the stability of capitalism from the outset, *maldistribution*.

We saw earlier that it was steady growth of aggregate output that largely neutralized the disturbing effect of inequality, shown by the steepness of the income and wealth pyramids in all capitalist nations. In order to prove that the issue is still topical, we must dispel a widespread myth. It concerns the idea that collective bargaining and the policy of entitlements have overcome gross inequality. In fact, even now the top 20 percent of family units in America receive 8 times the earned income of the lowest 20 percent. Moreover, the share of the lower 60 percent in total earnings fell between 1975 and 1985 by more than 10 percent. Thus transfer payments have at best prevented the distribution of spending power from becoming even more unequal. For this reason, as in the past, steady growth seems to be an indispensable condition for at least maintaining the prevailing distributional shares.

Yet in raising this issue we find ourselves confronted with a host of difficulties that make it doubtful whether, in the long run, even the new technological revolution can achieve the required rate of economic growth. The impediments of which we are speaking are *ecological*: the triad of worldwide population explosion, gradual exhaustion of essential material resources, and the pollution of the environment.

The significance of this complex is much wider than the context in which I introduce it here. Though slow in its advance, it may over the long run greatly modify mankind's style of life. All I want to demonstrate here is that, even under the most optimistic assumptions, it is an ecological factor that may ultimately block the economic growth of the West, as it is conventionally understood.

Let us admit that the first of the ecological tribulations—rapid population growth—can be traced to emancipatory progress, namely, to preventive medicine in the fight against infant mortality and epidemic diseases. In contrast, the other two factors must be seen as visitations of the sins of our liberal ancestors, whose ruthless exploitation of nature we have barely stopped imitating.

Perhaps the sudden shock in recognizing these dangers has misled experts and laymen alike in exaggerating their time scale and even their scope, and there may be technological solutions for most of them. This, however, will not eliminate the ultimate dangers that are *social* and *political*. They come to the fore once we relate the ecological issues to the demand of the underdeveloped two-thirds of mankind for economic emancipation. Even if their rate of population increase slows down, and if the potential treasures of the globe, augmented by more efficient utilization, should suffice to support worldwide industrialization, its *thermal effects* are likely to set strict limits to such a development. More specifically, in all probability the ecosphere cannot absorb the heat emitted by a relentless multiplication of energy input without catastrophic changes in the globe's climatic conditions. Thus an upper limit seems to exist for worldwide industrial growth, unless solar energy can be transformed internationally into the main source of power—at best a long-term process. Otherwise the share of the Third World in economic development can rise only at the expense of the presently advanced nations.

In concrete terms this means that the West, having lost its political and even military supremacy, will not be able to deny much longer a fair share of the world's material resources to the underprivileged. It is unlikely that the advanced nations will yield to moral persuasion. But they may encounter economic pressure as originally practiced by the oil cartel, not to speak of naked blackmail as a consequence of the proliferation of atomic weapons.

It stands to reason that such a shift in the balance of material wealth is bound to reduce the growth rate of the Western nations, if it does not impose a decline. As a consequence of such international redistribution, the demand for *intranational redistribution* will be stepped up, heightening the tensions created by a job-reducing technology.

THE FAILURE OF WELFARE GOVERNMENTS

In summing up we cannot evade a question that goes to the root of this inquiry. Considering the calamitous events of the recent past and the gloomy prospect of the socioeconomic evolution, can we maintain our expectation that we have entered a new stage of emancipation? Are we not troubled by ills that are worse than all the predicaments that beset capitalism in the past: growing maldistribution, an endemic cycle of inflation and deflation, a rising reserve army of unemployed seeking work, and even serious obstacles to economic growth, the main stabilizer in the past? Contrary to our insistence that rational control is capable of taming the impersonal destructive forces, is there after all a mechanism at work that, in analogy with Marx's general law of capitalist accumulation, rules our fate, spelling doom for the social and cultural heritage of the West?

A reassuring answer is not made easier when we examine the policies pursued by the political embodiment of planning, the welfare state. It was a laissez-faire government that finally grasped the nettle, whereas those committed to planning accepted mounting inflation almost to the end of their rule as if it were ordained by an inexorable law.

One might perhaps reify some of the extraneous shocks by subsuming the Vietnam War under the category of imperialism, or by interpreting the technological revolution as another stage in the relentless process of accumulation with rising organic composition of capital. But the response to these shocks did not issue from impersonal agents. It was a political decision that rejected taxation as the proper means of financing war and that abetted the wage-price spiral by a lax monetary policy. It has become a popular pastime for the victorious decontrollers to denounce an all-powerful but incompetent bureaucracy for those failures. What those failures really reflect was *political weakness on the part of the rulers of the welfare state* in the face of an ongoing struggle over distribution.

But we have not yet reached rock bottom. Why, we must ask, was the Reagan government more courageous in resolving that struggle by a radical policy of deflation? To find the answer, all we have to do is analyze the 30 percent of the potential electorate that put the Reagan administration into power, and compare it with that of the losing 25 percent. The winners had reason to believe that the burden of the deflationary policy would not fall on them, though the subsequent recession refuted that belief for many. But their opponents, with labor in the lead, had every reason to conceive of themselves as the true victims of deflation. What is even more important for an understanding of the passivity of the welfare governments is the fact that, at least initially, their partisans would have been the victims also of a timely stop of the wage-price spiral.

This, then, is the crux of the matter. What we have been witnessing is a *social conflict*, kept latent during the decades of economic expansion but brought into the open through a wrong financial handling of foreign policy and a speedup of domestic reforms beyond the limits of the national consensus. Fear of losing the confidence of their supporters by the timely redress of initial mistakes paralyzed the welfare governments when only a violation of the short-term interests of their friends could have restored stability and thus served everyone's long-term welfare.

Even if they gain more presidential victories, the decontrollers will hardly find themselves in a better position as time proceeds. Once the public realizes that laissez-faire will neither cure technological unemployment nor reverse a falling rate of growth, the votes in favor of intelligent planning should reappear. But whether such planning will succeed in solving the problems of the age depends not only on wise domestic and foreign policies, but also on a public that gives precedence to its long-term interests even at the cost of short-term sacrifices.

THE ROLE OF THE SUBJECTIVE FACTOR IN DESTABILIZATION

It is customary to discuss remedial political action in terms of institutions and institutional reform. But one can do so with any prospect of success only if one is aware that no institution is stronger than the *subjective forces* that support it—forces that translate into action the beliefs and aspirations of people, be they persons with political responsibility or nonpolitical groups and the individuals that compose them. In tranquil times we easily forget that institutions are only the crystallization of routinized behavior conforming to established rules. Because of their apparent perpetuity they assume an objective character, confronting individuals and groups by constraining them. But in turbulent times like ours the truth is forced upon us that the stability of institutions and the effectiveness of any public policy rest on the affirmation, more often unconscious than deliberate, of those they seek to control.

There we encounter what today creates the extreme of dialectic tension, and the one most difficult to resolve. Earlier in this essay I called the triumph of critical thought and its spread to every society, advanced or primitive, the most "subversive" force released by the recent transformation. I acclaimed it as a genuine emancipatory power to the extent to which it pushes aside outmoded traditions, prejudices, and superstitions that block the way to our accepting the responsibilities that new technologies, both material and social, have placed in our hands. But like *aqua regia* in chemistry, the same force threatens to attack the "gold" in our beliefs and aspirations that protect us from anomie.

This is not to deny that those beliefs and aspirations are themselves shaped by the prevailing natural and social framework. They might be different and easier to reconcile with one another, and with the requisites of emancipation, if the Western nations were not riven by class division, or had preserved some of the ideologies that in the past had appeased the underprivileged. But it is today's social framework within which we must operate. And within this framework it is the manifestations of the subjective factor, the motivations and behavior patterns of strategic groups—in a democracy, ultimately the majority of voters—that decide whether structural change results in a new order or in chaos. We must face the fact that, of all the revolutionary upheavals to which we have been exposed during this century, none has been more radical than the transmutations of the beliefs, incentives, and the ensuing mode of action of ordinary men and women.

Speaking of the West, with which we are mainly concerned, an almost unbridgeable gap separates those whose outlook on life and moral standards was formed in the conventions of the nineteenth century from those who reached maturity after World War II. To call this a generation gap misses the gravity of the break. What we witness resembles the clash between two civilizations, a clash that would not be less radical if the older generation had preserved the trimmings of youth.

Daniel Bell's *Contradictions of Capitalism* is largely devoted to a study of this clash. He rightly stresses the fact that all through the liberal era the ruling middle class, while practicing a materialist individualism in economic matters, shared a common culture. They upheld a strict code of mores in their personal relations and in their public dealings, a broad streak of hypocrisy notwithstanding. Opposition to this premodern heritage was confined to socially powerless cliques. No doubt, more has survived of those conservative mores than meets the eye and the ear. Still, the hedonism, if not nihilism, once extolled by an insignificant minority poses today as the authentic way of life of large and articulate groups of the young.

Responding to this with moralizing censure would be quite out of place, for more than one reason. The desire for instant gratification, incompatible as it is with genuine emancipation, is rooted in the awareness of seemingly unredeemable social injustice within and without, and in the loss of metapersonal beliefs under the constant threat of political catastrophe if not of physical annihilation. Moreover, the tendency to overrate the rewards of the moment and to blind oneself to the requirements of a viable future, to pursue short-term personal and factional interests at the expense of urgent public needs—in a word, the absence of communal responsibility— is not confined to the so-called counterculture. It is encroaching upon the mainstays of society: business and labor, the tillers of the soil and the professions, and not a small number of those who are in charge of the public interest.

We spoke earlier of the weakness of welfare governments. What this weakness ultimately reflects is the growing strength of various power blocs: the military-industrial complex, the multinational corporations, and many trade unions. Unlike past factions, these groups pursue their particular goals in the name of freedom—freedom of enterprise and of collective bargaining. The ensuing social structure is sometimes pictured as a new feudalism. More cogent is their analogy to the semiautonomous estates of the late Middle Ages. Like those, they more and more paralyze independent governmental operation, evoking as a reaction the *specter of a new autocracy* to restore national unity.

As was pointed out before, traditional mores that might restrain these tendencies have worn thin, and misuse of group liberty decomposes what is left of inherited standards of behavior. Their place is taken by hedonistic patterns, broadcast in rapidly changing fashion by the mass media. Thus a new meeting of minds is created, but one that enhances the advancing trend to privatization at the expense of public commitment. Perhaps the most striking symptom in the United States is the recent Protestant revival, replacing the former "social gospel" by a new evangelism with a message of extreme individualism. What it all amounts to is the steady erosion of the foundation of genuine freedom, a macro order supported by the vigilant consensus of an aware citizenry.

4   Balancing Freedom and Order: Some Historical Models

The time has come for us to advance beyond taking stock of what is and how it came about. Our task now is to discover *what should be* if the social process, in the face of all the countervailing tendencies, is to move toward a macro order in which the potential for egalitarian freedom can materialize. What this amounts to can best be grasped when we pinpoint once more the major failure of our generation, which has prevented us so far from coming to grips with the prerequisites of such a course. *This failure consists in our clinging to the institutions and attitudes we inherited from a prior stage of emancipation.* In order to overcome the frustrations of the present, a sociopolitical and sociopsychological transformation must be accomplished.

Very much aware of the prevailing political and cultural climate, I approach this task in a somewhat skeptical mood. And this all the more so because designing a new order must remain a utopian undertaking, unless the forces can be identified that will make such a design acceptable to those who are supposed to put it into practice.

In our introductory survey we gave a general, though abstract, account of some of the conditions on which a satisfactory juncture of freedom and order depends. This account must now be brought down to a more realistic level, which means that we shall have to be specific about the institutional and attitudinal changes required.

The prospect of coming up with practicable answers will be greatly strengthened if we can relate our present problems to some historical instances in which comparable issues were handled more or less successfully. Of course, we must not expect that an inquiry into events that mark an earlier stage of emancipation, or even antedate what we defined as such, offers lessons directly applicable to our present concerns. None of those precedents had to face challenges on a par with those that confront us today—to think only of the role that planning plays in the establishment of new institutions. And yet, by learning about the forces that in certain periods of the past helped to balance freedom and order, but also about other forces that upset such a balance, we shall meet under a different guise some of the agents that may determine our own future.

SOCIETAL CONSTRAINTS IN ANTIQUITY AND THE MIDDLE AGES

An obvious example to start with is the *Athenian polis* of the fifth century B.C., to which we have referred in passing. It is the earliest society known to us in which personal liberty of all "free" men sustained a community the political and cultural achievements of which still stand out as a "classical" experience. Not that the issues which arose in a tiny city-state with a population not exceeding that of a middle-sized modern town—a state in whose economy serfdom and slavery played a major role—can in any way compare with the problems of a modern national state. But if we can trust the literary documents bequeathed to us, we have there a striking example of the role of societal constraints in safeguarding freedom.

In this respect Pericles' famous funeral oration, as reported in Thucydides' *History of the Peloponnesian War*, is very enlightening. Some modern interpreters have read into it the glorification of almost unlimited personal freedom. And indeed the spirit of John Stuart Mill's *On Liberty* seems to have found an early voice when we read: " . . . as we give free play to all in our public life, so we carry the same spirit on to our daily relations with one another. We have no black looks or angry words for our neighbor if he enjoys himself in his own way. . . . " But Pericles continues: " . . . open and friendly in our private intercourse, in our public acts we keep strictly within the control of law. We acknowledge the restraint of reverence; we are obedient to whomsoever is set in authority, and to the laws, more especially "those unwritten laws that bring upon the transgressor of them the *reprobation* of general sentiment." (Benjamin Jowett's translation. Italics added).

Not that the stability of the macro order, to apply the term introduced earlier, was totally entrusted to those unwritten laws. In our quotation the contribution of the *written law* together with *constitutional authority* (and thus enforced conformity) is equally stressed. Moreover, the public freedom that the Athenian constitution bestowed on every free person was hedged in by the same societal constraints that limited private behavior. "Our citizens," continues Pericles, "attend both to public and private duties, and do not allow their own affairs to interfere with their knowledge of the city's. We differ from other states in regarding the man who holds aloof from public life not as quiet but as useless" (same translation). In other words, public freedom was not conceived as a *right* to be made use of arbitrarily, but as a *duty* watched over by the same "general sentiment."

We shall never know whether what Thucydides tells us here describes the real state of affairs, making the constitution of the city, in Aristotle's words, a way of life. But we know enough of the subsequent breakdown to trace the destruction of the polis to the end of spontaneous conformity in rising factionalism.

LIBERAL ENGLAND AS A PARADIGM OF SPONTANEOUS CONFORMITY

A rather different but still relevant case is the medieval bifurcation of secular and ecclesiastical jurisdiction. In referring to it earlier, we stressed a conformist discipline that limited for quite some time both rulers and ruled in the pursuit of worldly interests. William James, deploring the moral slackness of his generation, looked for a substitute for war. Those distant ages found it in the universal belief in heaven and hell.

Still, as is true of the ancient city, neither feudalism nor the guild system of the medieval town can be compared with the structure of modern democracies. The problem of mere size invalidates such a comparison. Rousseau, a staunch advocate of societal controls, was convinced that they could be effective only in small political units. And indeed, at first sight it seems impossible that spontaneous conformity could develop in a mass society. Devoid of the personal relations that in an ancient or medieval town brought most members into almost daily contact, separated if not alienated by an ever increasing division of functions that splits even the individual into more and more "roles," what force could sustain a "general will" on a national scale?

A surprising and altogether affirmative answer is provided by a phase of *recent English history*, beginning roughly with Disraeli's Reform Bill of 1867 and extending to the years just after World War II. Its significance lies in the fact that we deal here with a large-scale industrial society that somehow succeeded in reconciling a maximum of public freedom with the requisites of a stable macro order. A thorough examination of this paradigm will be our next task.

The task is not easy. The forces that combined to make the system work defy strict conceptualization. They were located in a region of tacit rapport that resists precise analysis. On the other hand, the overt facts are well known and have been amply commented upon, mainly by foreigners trying to fathom the English "national character." Our aim is less ambitious, and concerned with one issue only. We want to uncover the reasons why, during the era in question, England came nearer to stability under self-government than any contemporaneous Western society.

But from the outset a warning is in order. The reader had better lay aside all he or she knows of contemporary England and its current political and economic troubles. We are going to speak of a brief era that seems to be irrevocably past, even if one may hope that some of its characteristics linger underneath. Certainly the peaceful revolution the country passed through in the decade after the war bore an impressive testimony to that heritage.

THE PARADOX OF ENGLISH CONFORMITY

Choosing England as the paradigm of a society relying largely on spontaneous conformity, and thus on mainly societal constraints, confronts us with a real paradox. To see this, we need only list some of the institutional conditions that, in the abstract, appear as indispensable for creating a spirit of conformity. At a minimum there seem to be three such conditions: external security reducing the need for central regulation; a fair degree of equality, both economic and social; and a wide sharing of responsibility in public life.

During the period under consideration, the first and third of those conditions were certainly present. Geography and a powerful navy provided the first. With regard to a wide sharing of public responsibility, a high degree of administrative and judicial decentralization and a long tradition of voluntary association—from the chapel meeting through trade unionism to the organization of the political parties—opened extensive opportunities for public activity. This was reinforced in the economic realm through the practice of laissez-faire by small and medium-sized enterprises.

What seemed, however, to disqualify England's claim to representing a free macro order was the fact that it was the most class-ridden society of the West. A few stark figures illustrate the then prevailing *economic inequality*. Whereas, during the period considered, the upper 5 percent of the population in the United States or in Germany appropriated about 30 percent of the national income, in Britain they took 45 percent. Two-thirds of the British national wealth—compared with one-third in Germany—was in the hands of people owning more than £5,000. Land ownership and ground property in the cities was the privilege of the aristocracy and the upper middle class, with 80 percent of the land in the possession of a few thousand persons.

This flagrant economic inequality was matched by *social disparity*. Perhaps only in Germany beyond the Elbe could one find such crass traces of a former feudal order—not in the political organization of the country, especially after the power of the House of Lords had been curtailed, but in the manner in which the aristocracy occupied the highest representative positions as a matter of course. And the gulf that separated the middle classes from the "working classes" was certainly as wide as in any Continental country, and much wider than in the United States.

Supporting this class structure was a truly elitist educational system. The intellectual and moral preparation for leadership in politics and business was entrusted to exclusive private schools—in England called public schools—and to the "ancient" universities at Oxford and Cambridge. To mention a small but characteristic symptom of cultural elitism, where else was snobbery driven to the point where traces of a regional dialect passed for an inferior status rather than for a sign of origin?

Judging by our abstract principles, no country in the entire world of modern capitalism seemed better suited as a battleground for a Marxian class struggle. The least one would expect was disaffection on the part of those groups whose social advancement was thwarted by the prevailing order. And indeed, did not these tensions explode in the general strike of the 1920s?

But now the plot thickens. Can we imagine in a similar crisis the U.S. or German police joining the strikers in a football match? Or the German crown prince heading the subscription list in aid of the strikers' wives and children, as did the prince of Wales? There we have a telling illustration of our general thesis, though we are far from suggesting that the victims of the prevailing class structure accepted their fate in meek resignation. In fact, Britain's modern history, from the Reform Bill of 1832 to the inauguration of the first Labour government, from the free trade controversy to Lloyd George's social reforms, was a continuous struggle for political and economic equalization.

It was the manner in which those struggles were fought that revealed an underlying solidarity. After a brief spell of scattered violence in the early industrial period, the combat was waged from below with the weapons of reformism—in the House of Commons, through the actions of trade unions and cooperatives. Resistance from above never took any counterrevolutionary form. The concessions made—first on the part of the aristocracy to the rising bourgeoisie, later to Labour on the part of Conservatives and Liberals alike—achieved compromises acceptable to all. To preclude false idealization, it must be stressed that those bargains in the long run proved advantageous also to the apparent losers. The parties to those bargains did not play a zero-sum game, where one party's gain would have been the other party's loss. Both aristocracy and middle class found ample compensation for concessions in the benefits reaped from Britain's advanced position at home and abroad.

In using the rallying cry of the French Revolution as our standard, we can say that English society during the era under consideration represented a sort of "*national fraternity*." But we must strip away from such a notion all romantic associations, and understand such brotherhood as a very sober relationship. What it amounts to is that the contacts of daily life and the political tug-of-war were conducted in the temperate mood of a unity of purpose. Generous readiness to help and even self-sacrifice had their part in it, as much as the tenacious insistence of individuals and groups on what they regarded as their rights. But two extremes were disparaged: pursuit of private concerns at the expense of the elementary interests of the nation as a whole, and total absorption of the person in an imagined superorganism. Private and public life moved midway between an emphasis on individuation and passive submission to some leadership.

I said earlier that the ruling code of behavior is difficult to formulate in precise terms. Decency and fairness, sportmanship, never hitting below the belt, being a good loser, above all an instinct for "what is not done"—these are the terms used by the actors themselves to describe an attitude to which all classes were suppoesd to conform, and by and large did conform. Some observers spoke of a "Christian spirit" permeating public life. We shall have occasion to say more about the historic role of Christian tradition and the lasting influence of the churches of all denominations on life and work. But one cannot call modern Britain a Christian society, unless emphasis is on social activity rather than on doctrine and spiritual exultation.

THE ROLE OF EDUCATION

Against this background we shall examine more closely some of the institutions we have been touching on and their effect on personal freedom. By what social technique was the ruling code of behavior established and passed on from one generation to the next? The obvious answer is "*education*," the term taken in its widest possible interpretation. While certainly not underestimating formal instruction and training, we should be aware that the climate of public opinion and the ruling conventions are the product of many factors, largely of nonrational ones. Family life and the manners and morals supporting it, the church as both a religious and a social institution, newspapers and other media of communication, works of art, and especially literary expression in poetry and fiction are some of the formative agents of thinking and feeling, the subtle impress of which reaches deeper and is longer lasting than the yield of rational schooling. It so happened that during that period all those influences converged in inculcating a set of values that strengthened the conformist spirit. Even when social critics spoke with voices as different as those of Dickens, Ruskin, and Shaw, they did so on behalf of the same value system and in opposition to its hypocritical perversion.

As far as formal education is concerned, a broadcast during the interwar period by Prime Minister Stanley Baldwin is characteristic. He admonished the graduating classes of all British high schools: "Never be logical!" It was of course an elliptical statement referring to a tradition in which character ranked above intellect.

To an outsider it may sound strange that even the leading universities, Oxford and Cambridge, in some way adopted the same principle. At no time did those universities serve as intellectual training centers in the French or German style—they were rearing grounds of a social type. Fred Clark, the leading British educator during the interwar period, put it this way: From the eighteenth century on, classical humanist education, apparently concerned with handing down a cultural tradition, in fact developed into the training for a vocation—that of rulers.

As this cultural tradition was interpreted, it indeed showed some affinity with the world in which the student lived, and even more with the stage on which he was supposed to act later on. Especially the "aristocratic democracy" of classical Athens was taken to reflect not only the manner in which England chose its leaders but also the sovereign independence with which those leaders exercised their power so long as they retained the confidence of their constituencies. Most important was the image of the *polis* as model for a society in which the unwritten laws of a commonly accepted convention shaped the maturing character. The typical product of such an education was neither a scholar nor a specialized expert, but a "gentleman amateur" imbued with the moral ideals of the age, preparing himself for the world in which he was to assume leadership.

All this seems only to confirm what was said earlier about the elitist structure of English higher education. Still, an important proviso must be added. During the later part of the period we are contemplating, and especially during the interwar years, the social stratification of the student body changed considerably. On the one

hand, the "provincial" universities, with their emphasis on specialized training, attracted one-third of all students. A vast system of
scholarships brought increasing numbers of graduates from institutions other than public schools to Oxford and Cambridge. Thus
the traditional upper class was diluted with a growing admixture
of middle-class and even working-class students. It has been said
that nowhere else could a talented man or woman climb the educational ladder as easily as in England after World War I—but at a
price. What happened was a repetition of the process of social assimilation through which, a century earlier, Rugby and other
"modern" public schools "domesticated" the new industrial middle
class to the standards of upper-class behavior. In the same manner,
when the gates of the older universities opened, opportunities were
provided for gifted persons willing to adopt the conventions ruling
there, and to be received into a higher social class.

Sometimes this system has been denounced as an insidious attempt at drawing away potential leaders from the underprivileged strata. But is should not be forgotten that some fluidity of
the class structure worked both ways—in the upward direction
through a wide sweep of the Honors List, but also in the downward direction by the stepping down of the younger members of
the aristocracy to the level of "commoners." There was more than
a grain of truth in Friedrich Engels' sardonic comment that "This
most bourgeois of all nations is apparently aiming at the possession
of a bourgeois aristocracy and a bourgeois proletariat as well as a
bourgeoisie."

THE "ENDS" OF ENGLISH CONFORMITY

The "forty religions but only one sauce" about which Voltaire
quipped contributed a good deal to the homogeneity of mores within
a well-defined social stratification. As was indicated, it was social
activism rather than theological profoundity that made the Free
Churches the center of personal life of the lower middle class and
the workers. From the sermon down to the children's parties and
the whist drives, they filled the leisure time of those groups, bringing them, on neutral ground, into contact with the social class above
and below them. But no less important was the watch over the

social balance on the part of the established church, which sometimes openly sided with the masses even against Parliament.

A special role in the maintenance of this delicate balance fell to
the *intelligentsia*. In every modern society this is the "critical" stratum, in its radical form typified by the French Encyclopedists of
the eighteenth century or the intellectual revolutionaries of nine-
teenth-century Russia. One looks in vain for a parallel movement
in British social history. Not that the representative groups were
obedient servants of the conformist tradition. After all, groups such
as the Philosophical Radicals or, later, the Fabians fought their way
into recognition by rewriting fundamental rules of the social code.
But characteristically those movements were always only one step
ahead of public opinion. Though they kept the social process dynamic, they reduced its pace to one of gradualism. They showed
little of that passion for controversy and for pushing an argument
to its limits which was so popular among their Continental opposite
numbers. That the depths should not be stirred up showed only
too clearly in most of the artistic products of the Victorian age. It
was not much different in theology and philosophy. Cardinal New-
man's conversion to Roman Catholicism was a demonstration against
the prevailing doctrinal laxity. Oxford idealism with Green and
Bosanquet laid a philosophical foundation for the liberal practice.
The Continental observer saw with astonishment that the method
of compromise could be applied in intellectual discourse. Even
Darwin never publicly abandoned Christianity, which in private
he denounced as a "damnable doctrine."

These last remarks imply some of the *ends* to the attainment of
which the different strata of English society "spontaneously" con-
formed. So far as the individual was concerned, the aim was the
molding of a peculiar character, striving in its highest manifestation
for an ethical humanism while imbuing the common man with the
plainer virtues of self-reliance, fellowship, and respect for tradition.
Moreover—and this proved decisive—this code was by no means
frozen. The era we are considering was a period of gradual transformation—on the one hand an attempt at domesticating the cruder
instincts and passions, on the other hand a loosening of religious
and even sexual taboos by interpreting the unconventional as the
truly moral (vide John Stuart Mill or George Eliot). But the true
dynamics of this "code of manners" (as Edmund Burke called it)

showed in the transmutation of personal values into *social reform*, an effect greatly facilitated by the extroverted nature of the personal code, which stressed behavior rather than belief.

This interaction of personal striving with the aspirations of large groups helps us to understand how, in contrast with Continental experience, social reform in England cut across class and even party lines. Striking instances are "Tory socialism" and the abiding loyalty to the Liberal Party of many members of the working classes far into the twentieth century. Shifting alliances of only vaguely defined party formations rather than extraparliamentary pressures were the engines of social progress. In the middle of the nineteenth century, Disraeli had spoken of the "two nations" into which industrial capitalism threatened to divide the country. A generation later—not least due to his own electoral reforms—the remaining social conflicts were generally regarded as open to gradual solution.

What was said earlier about the economic and social inequalities that prevailed during the same period is ample proof of the conservative nature of the reform movement. What yet preserved the spirit of conformity was the steady economic improvement of all classes, even though the social pyramid extended itself instead of shrinking.

THE HISTORICAL ROOTS OF ENGLISH CONFORMITY

In order to avoid any romantic idealization, it is necessary to survey briefly the main stages leading up to the period we have just described. We must start with *geography*. The significance of Britain's insularity has often been stressed, but mainly under the aspect of military security. Its isolation was equally important for domestic policy. It made it possible to play the sociopolitical game of attack-resistance-compromise without external interference. Of course, this was possible only within an otherwise unified nation. Therefore the Norman conquest must be seen as a stroke of luck, because in all likelihood only a foreign conqueror could have checked political feudalism so early, laying the foundation for a *central government*. How stable those foundations were became clear 150 years later in the baronial struggle terminating in the Magna Carta. Of course, it is a product of fanciful hindsight to call Magna Carta the origin of English democracy; it was an affair between the feudal lords and the king. Its real significance stands out when it is compared with a simultaneous event on the Continent. At the very same time that a viable unification of the nation was achieved in England, a compact between the German emperor and the principal magnates on German soil formalized the dissolution not only of the empire but also of the German nation. In Britain the central power was placed under some control, but as such left untouched.

Within this firm political framework the long road started that led to the growing influence of the towns, to the Puritan revolution and the Glorious Revolution, the Reform Bill of 1832, and the electoral reforms of the last 100 years. This process marks the *steady rise of the urban middle class*, not only politically but also economically. When feudal land rents still predominated on the Continent, the main source of national wealth in England had long been commerce and the production of raw materials for the urban economy. Even the enclosures, rightly deplored for their detrimental effect on the agrarian population, destroyed a key position of feudalism. So had, earlier, the Wars of the Roses and the expropriation of the church.

England's predominant position in international trade since the eighteenth century, its head start in industrialization coinciding with a steadily expanding colonial empire, provided the material basis for the gradual ascent of its poorer classes. It also offered an outlet for nonconforming adventurers and, above all, ample economic compensation for the gradual loss of predominance of an already "bourgeoisified" aristocracy. What is striking and without equal in any other European country is the steady rise of the middle classes from the height of the Middle Ages to the apex of the imperial realm in the early twentieth century. As a consequence these classes carried many of the features of the medieval burgher over into the modern age.

This showed very distinctly during the one era that seemed to break with that tradition, the cultural renaissance under Elizabeth I and James I. The foreign observer is tempted to judge this era mainly by aesthetic standards. But the representative guild circles by no means regarded the lack of self-restraint of the major characters of the Elizabethan drama as an expression of the true English spirit. Growing resentment of the "pagan" *zeitgeist* exploded in the

Puritan revolution. Subsequently the Restoration swept Puritan radicalism from the surface of society for more than a century. But it reemerged in secularized form during the Victorian age, mainly under the impact of the industrial North in opposition to the spirit of "merrie" England. At the same time, the reformed public schools succeeded in amalgamating aristocratic and middle-class traditions in the image of the "gentleman"—a modern version of the medieval patrician.

THE PROBLEM OF FREEDOM

So much for conformity and its historical role. But what about *freedom?* In answering this question, we should, first of all, remember that, by common agreement, post-Cromwellian Britain has been the West's promoter of *public freedom*. Certainly the Reform Bill of 1832 started a century of uninterrupted progress in extending such freedom to the entire adult population, ultimately transforming Britain into a genuine democracy. There are today none of the checks and balances with which the Constitutional Convention tried to protect U.S. society from what Alexander Hamilton called "the ambition, vindictiveness and rapacity" of men. And yet Britain's political stability remained unimpaired during that critical period when the countries on both the European and the American continent were afflicted by revolutions and civil war. Not only did government in Britain turn more and more into self-government, but political controls played altogether a minor role, while the economic process was left almost entirely to the autonomy of free market relations. Thus the Englishman of that era seemed fully justified in the belief that he lived in the freest country on the globe.

But what about *private freedom?* So long as we confine ourselves to human and civil rights, the answer must be equally affirmative. Ever since the passing of the Habeas Corpus Act and the Declaration of Rights in the late seventeenth century, an inviolable inner sanctum of privacy has been assured, well symbolized in the slogan that an Englishman's home is his castle. And yet, whereas the reign of public liberty has been universally acknowledged by native and foreign commentators, when it comes to assessing private liberty, opinions are sharply divided. Outsiders almost unanimously agree with Mill that though the yoke of law is lightest in England, "the yoke of opinion is perhaps heavier . . . than in most countries of Europe." In other words, even if the widest range of individual activity was exempt from political controls, that range was beset by informal societal constraints.

One could fill a volume with the critical remarks laid down by Continental observers in travel books, studies of national character, and even philosphical treatises. All agree with what Heinrich Heine early in the nineteenth century called the "colossal uniformity" of personal relations, even if no one else went as far as the Belgian Renier a century later in asking: "The English, are they Human?" For reasons that we shall presently examine more closely, it was the Germans who based a philosophy and sociology of culture on the alleged contrast between English liberty and "deutsche Freiheit.'

Most interesting of all is a comment by the German philosopher Max Scheler. In a study written during World War I, he first of all stressed what seemed to him special English "virtues": strong devotion to public liberty, traditional distrust of political controls, a rare capacity for promoting collective goals through voluntary associations. But he found on the other side of the ledger thick-headedness, narrow-mindedness, and, above all, a lack of freedom in matters that concern the mind and the soul—in other words, genuine private freedom. In stressing those opposite poles he seemed only to repeat what others had said before. But what gives his reflections an original flavor is his conclusion that those "vices" are the necessary counterpart of the "virtues." He even speaks of a "tragic law of human nature," according to which the scope of private liberty must always be in inverse proportion to the scope of public liberty.

"DIE DEUTSCHE FREIHEIT"

To clarify this puzzling issue, a brief digression into German *Geistesgeschichte* may be helpful. What is this "liberty of mind and soul" that the typical German is supposed to enjoy, and the typical Englishman is said to be without?

An enlightening guide can be found in the famous essay *On Liberty* by John Stuart Mill, rightly considered the most forceful literary defense of what we have defined as private freedom. In making his plea, Mill writes in a tradition that reaches back to Milton and includes other noted thinkers of British extraction. But in looking for an intellectual ally Mill turned to a very differenct source: a tract entitled *Ideen zu einem Versuch, die Grenzen der Wirksamkeit des Staates zu bestimmen* (*Spheres and Duties of Government*), written by Wilhelm von Humboldt, a Prussian statesman and philosopher in the post-Napoleonic era.

What characterizes Humboldt and Mill is a *specific function they assign to private liberty.* Noninterference of government and society with individual thinking and acting is for them not an end in itself but a means to a quite peculiar goal. They want man to be free to pursue his own good in his own way, because only thus can he develop his "individuality." Citing Humboldt, Mill pronounces that "The end of man . . . is the highest and most harmonious development of his powers to a complete and consistent whole." Therefore, "The object toward which *every human being must ceaselessly direct his efforts* . . . is the individuality of power and development" (italics added). For this there are "two requisites, freedom and variety of situations; and from the union of these arise individual vigor and manifold diversity, which combine themselves in originality."

"*Individuality culminating in originality*"—how strange that a British voice should sound a message that was the outgrowth of a very different tradition. Far from stating an idiosyncratic view, Humboldt spoke authentically for the classical age of German literature and philosophy. Two well-known pronouncements of representative thinkers will illustrate the point. In Goethe's *West-Eastern Divan* we read:

> Volk und Knecht und Überwinder,
> Sie gestehn zu jeder Zeit:
> Höchstes Glück der Erdenkinder
> Sei nur die Persönlichkeit.

This was rather awkwardly translated by Edward Dowden as

> The slave, the lord of victories,
> the crowd, whene'er you ask, confess
> In sense of personal being lies
> A child of earth's chief happiness.

And Kant, in the *Groundwork of the Metaphysic of Morals*, proclaims, "If there should be an absolute value, it could only be found in the individual as an end-in-itself."

One might be tempted to dismiss these ideas and the notion of a "deutsche Freiheit" derived from them as ideological freaks. I hesitate to do so because these speculations reflect a *reality*—a reality that by its very contrast throws new light on the English tradition.

This reality was the complete withdrawal of the German *Bürger* into the realm of private freedom since the end of the Middle Ages leaving the political destiny of the nation in the hands of the rulers of absolute states and their bureaucracies. It was a "mechanical clamp" imposed from above that held together a society whose consensus from below never reached beyond regional limits.

Goethe gave this antagonism a classical formulation when he wrote (Xenion 96):

> Deutscher Nationalcharakter
> Zur Nation euch zu bilden, ihr hoffet es,
> Deutsche, vergebens;
> Bildet, ihr könnt es, dafür freier zu
> Menschen euch aus!

> German National Character
> Germans, in vain do you hope to form
> yourselves as a nation;
> What you are able to do is
> to become freer as men!

This interplay between authoritarian government and the privatization of its subjects is illustrated by the peculiar role of absolutism in Germany. In the West absolutism represented a brief interlude between the breakdown of the medieval order and the rise of constitutional government. The alliance of the absolute monarch with the urban middle classes against agrarian feudalism provided first the economic, and then the political, springboard from which the bourgeoisie rose to dominance, displacing its former patron by more or less violent revolutions. Moreover, in Britain and France it was the absolute monarch who at an early time achieved national unification.

None of this is true of the central European territory that, during the Middle Ages, formed the center of the Holy Roman Empire. From the thirteenth century on, this center dissolved into small sovereign principalities, amounting to more than 100 around the year 1500. It is in these principalities that a petty absolutism developed which allied itself with the agrarian interests of a refeudalized aristocracy, remaining aloof or even in conflict with the politically autonomous cities.

We focus on the early sixteenth century because that period is significant for the rise of the idea of a "deutsche Freiheit." This was the moment when a spiritual seal was placed on the sociopolitical structure that could be called a "German nation" only in linguistic terms. This was accomplished in Martin Luther's tracts *On the Freedom of Christian Man* and *Of Secular Authority and Our Obedience to It*. There, in unmistakable terms, the innermost recess of the private person—his soul as saved by Christ's mercy—was designated as the true seat of human freedom. In contrast with this, the body and the external world at large were denounced as the dominion of Satan, to be kept under control by an autocratic government. Its instrument, an all-powerful bureaucracy, should certainly be guided by moral principles. But failing this, there was no right of resistance to an unjust government, the scourge ordained by God as punishment for our sins.

It would be absurd—though it has sometimes been done—to make Luther responsible for the sociopolitical conditions on German territory, which his writings reflect so faithfully. His responsibility lies in the attempt to *justify* the actual state of affairs by invoking religious principles, and thus to strengthen the political powers in their persistence.

There lie the roots of that quietism, if not enthusiastic applause, with which the average German of modern times accepted a proudly avowed Machiavellian policy, domestic and foreign, to which Thomas Mann's *Thoughts in Wartime*, written at the outbreak of World War I, bear such a grotesque testimony. Thus arose that Janus-faced image of a sincere cosmopolitanism wrestling with extreme nationalism, of a political romanticism joined to brute *realpolitik*, of reactionary conservatism confronting revolutionary experimentation in the arts and sciences. For this ambivalence the slogan "Potsdam versus Weimar" has been coined—a dubious label suggesting that Weimar, the symbol of "poets and thinkers," was

all "good" and Potsdam, the symbol of military autocracy, all "bad."
In truth a political Potsdam was the very precondition for an apolitical Weimar.

The same polarity was the breeding ground of that fierce class
struggle after industrialization had spread, a struggle that did not
have its equal in any other Western country. In this way the ruling
class tried to exclude many millions of citizens from the political
life of the nation, because as socialists they were "fellows without
a fatherland."

With all this one must not overlook certain forces that made for
some degree of social cohesion. But they bore a merely local or
regional character, expressing themselves in folkways and mores of
different strata without any pervading *national* style of thinking and
acting. No equivalent of the reality-shaping types of "gentlemen"
and "citoyen" grew out of the recesses of the German personality,
which in Fichte's term cultivated "Innerlichkeit" (inwardness).

At first it might appear that the idea of "Volkstum," so central
for the Romantic movement in the early nineteenth century, sig-
nified a break with this individualistic tradition. But the "Volk" in
the Romantic understanding was a nonpolitical, ultimately biological entity. As such it was pliable material for the form-giving power
of the state, as was demonstrated only too strongly a century later
in the onslaught of the "Herrenrasse."

No wonder this extreme subjectivism and particularism frus-
trated all attempts at political reform on a national scale—first after
the Napoleonic Wars, then in the abortive revolution of the "professors" in 1848, and, most tragically, in the self-destruction of the
Weimar Republic. Neither Bismarck's constitution for the new
German Reich, which retained much of the autocratic Prussian tradition, nor the belated introduction of parliamentary rule in 1919
changed the essentials. There are many reasons for its failure, but
not the least was the insistence of the parliamentary parties on remaining "*Weltanschauungsparteien*," unwilling to compromise the pu-
rity of irreconcilable principles.

It is only fair to acknowledge that the very forces which brought
political disaster served as a creative stimulus in the realms of art
and science, literature and philosophy. In all those fields German
achievements at least equaled those of their Western neighbors—
and surpassed them in music, the very art of "Innerlichkeit." And

the absence of communal bonds provided a fertile ground for radical thinkers like Marx, Nietzsche, and Freud, whose critical insights escaped the society-bound intelligentsia across the Channel.

But the picture is incomplete unless we try to assess not only the political but also the cultural failings of this German tradition. It was apolitical in any but a millennial sense, but it was also *elitist* in the extreme. When Humboldt spoke of individuality of power and development as the goal toward which every human being must ceaselessly direct his efforts, the "human beings" he had in mind were, of course, the "Gebildeten," the elite of the educated. What this elite thought of the common man, another poet of the classical age, August von Platen, made abundantly clear: "Germany—a few hardy swimmers in a sea of nonsense," thus highlighting the unbridgeable gulf that separated the highbrow minority from the lowbrow majority. Such arrogance was matched by the contempt that the true power holders, army and bureaucracy, felt for the same minority.

This leads us back to Scheler's "tragic law of human nature," according to which private freedom and public freedom stand in irreconcilable conflict. Tragic or not, the lesson he points to throws light on the essential difference between English and German tradition. It yields the insight that no large-scale society can entrust its fate to self-government, unless societal constraints keep the conduct of its members within definite limits. In a nutshell: *The price of public freedom is self-constraint*.

CONFORMITY AS A THREAT AND A RESCUE

Violation of this principle has not been the exclusive bane of Germany—a survey of French history would have provided us with some striking illustrations, though without the philosophical rationalization so typical of German *Geistesgeschichte*. What, however, leads us back to our main story is the fact that more and more, such violations became a distinctive mark of England after World War I. Such violations were not the willful act of any social group, but a consequence of a change in objective conditions.

Geographical isolation, early centralization defeating political feudalism, a head start in commercial and industrial capitalism, an empire on which the sun truly did not set—this was, as we saw, the historical background and the environment in which the communal spirit grew and, by its successful operation, steadily reinforced itself. After the end of World War I those conditions had largely been obliterated—by the airplane, the rise of technologically superior competitors, the beginning of decolonization, and the transformation of the empire into a commonwealth of sovereign nations.

Earlier we saw that, during the liberal era, the economic realm was the first to abandon the political controls of the past in favor of unconstrained individualistic competition. Now, 100 years later, the need for restructuring and even relocating British industry in accord with a radically changed world market urgently called for planning, because the required scope and tempo of readjustment went far beyond what could be achieved by the trial and error of private decision making. Absence of a concerted policy resulted in a lingering depression, which accompanied the adjustment process up to the outbreak of World War II. This was bound to sharpen the conflict between capital and labor, all the more so as the parties to the dispute fundamentally disagreed about the course that adjustment should take. Even though the general strike of 1926 was conducted in a spirit of nonviolence, it was a general strike after all, revealing a disaffection that the preceding decades of expansion had only neutralized.

In this rougher social climate other forces, which formerly had contributed to conformity, turned divisive. The intellectual attacks on the iniquities of the system—formerly a target of a reformist gradualism—now raised doubts about the viability of capitalism as such. The inherited "code of manners" was openly defied in theory and practice by ever widening strata. One must not forget that, during the heyday of societal constraints, the average individual had to pay a price in the form of psychological repression, as biographies and novels of the Victorian era amply document. With the end of expansion the rewards of such repression in terms of domestic peace and material progress rapidly shrank. Secularization of outlook, a loosening of family ties, and a laxer sexual morality invaded even the lower and most conventional strata of society. At the other end of the social scale, the Oxford Student Union resolved never again to fight for king and country.

Perhaps the most powerful forces sapping the conformist spirit were beyond the control of any single nation, signifying the world-wide breakup of former constraints. Among them was the rising demand for equality. This was bound to conflict with some of the ends that the conformist spirit had willy-nilly sustained in Britain: the plutocratic social pyramid and an imperialist foreign policy. Enough has been said about the former, though the full divisive effect showed only in the decades following World War II. But a word should be added about British imperialism.

British colonial administration, when judged by efficiency and fairness, was probably second to none. But a traditional aloofness in dealing with "natives," and even with "foreigners" generally, created deep resentment in the educated strata of the dependencies, some of which could boast a civilization much older than that of their colonial masters. In a more subtle way this was even true of the relations with the dominions, which during this critical period attained full sovereignty. So one can say that the imperial spirit itself was a solvent of the imperial structure.

So far we have argued as if maintenance of the traditional spirit of conformity would have been desirable even under the new circumstances. But we stressed at the very beginning of our deliberations that, with the rise of new criteria of thought and action, a prevailing state of conformity is likely to lose its legitimate function and to turn into an obstacle for the transformation of institutions and attitudes. This was certainly true of England during this critical period.

A crucial feature of the social code during the nineteenth century had been its dynamic nature, shaping as well as yielding to the pressure of public opinion, and thus neatly balancing the progressive and the conservative forces. This dynamic slackened first in the economic sphere. Britain's complacent resting on past laurels permitted the United States and Germany to overake it in technology and industrial organization. Many of the difficulties that beset the British economy during the interwar period were due to an economic conservatism, shared equally by capital and labor, creating a productivity gap that has not been closed even today.

Still more damaging was the political paralysis during the 1930s, which by a hair's breadth missed destroying the nation's life and liberty. One can certainly blame successive governments for having

failed to give the nation the leadership that the growing international dangers required. Whatever motives were hiding behind this
passivity—not least the hope that the dictators on the Continent
might neutralize, if not destroy, each other—it is only fair to state
that the official attitude of "muddling through" faithfully reflected
the mood of the nation at large, and in particular that of organized
labor. It was the mood in which Richard Wagner makes the giant
Fafner answer his challenger Siegfried: "I rest in possession, let
met go on sleeping."

And yet this is not the whole truth. Though such passivity lasted
far into the phase of the "phony war," a most dynamic mode of
national conformity sprang up once the German guns across the
Channel and the German planes over the island itself brought the
reality of the situation home to every man, woman, and child. One
may well insist that had such a dynamic mode prevailed a quin-
quennium earlier, the emergency could have been forestalled. As it
was, this spirit saw the nation victoriously through against overwhelming odds.

It is well worth remembering the major events in which the new
spirit took form. I am not thinking primarily of the formation of a
national government, nor of that student generation which, having
only a few years earlier rejected king and country, now manned
the Spitfires and Hurricanes to which so many were to owe so
much. What in our context is paramount were some radical institutional changes. At the height of the Battle of France, both houses
of Parliament unanimously passed a bill that, in Churchill's words,
gave "the government practically unlimited power over the life, liberty and property of His Majesty's subjects in Great Britain . . .
the Minister of Labor was empowered to direct every one to perform any service required. . . . Controls of all establishments, including banks, were imposed—excess profits were to be taxed at
100%." For the duration of the war, all major inequalities were
annulled.

Not outside the Soviet Union—certainly not in Germany—was
a comparable symbiosis established among all classes of the population, and this by a grandiose demonstration of public freedom.
Catastrophe as the midwife of a new spontaneous conformity—is
this the ultimate lesson of a century of English experience?

A Viable Tomorrow

We shall try to answer the question that ended Chapter 4 in due course, after having placed it in the proper context. We already pointed to this context when we stressed the need for a sociopolitical and sociopsychological transformation, through which the frustrations that today block the approach to the emancipatory goal can be overcome. To the task of elaborating such a program of planned transformation this and the subsequent three chapters will be devoted.

Our first topic is *the minimum of institutional changes required*. In this and the next chapter we are going to develop the *instrumental conditions* for such changes. This term denotes the *means suitable to attain the end*, which we have defined as egalitarian freedom in a social order that performs above the critical threshold of instability.

In this instrumental inquiry we are not yet concerned with the *force that can actually transform the prevailing institutions*. This will be the subject of the subsequent two chapters. But our survey of the major events of postwar history has taught us that, in the absence of the constraints of an earlier era, this force, namely, goal-adequate behavior, cannot be taken for granted. The measures required to ensure such behavior, and thus a new quasi stability of the system at large will be discussed in chapters 7 and 8.

This raises a host of new questions. First we must discover what kind of controls will prove adequate. No less important is the guarantee that those to whom the designing and the execution of such controls is entrusted will keep within the bounds of what is required. In other words, we shall have to answer the time-honored query: *Who controls the controllers?*

We must not start on this complex undertaking without introducing some provisos that simplify our task to some extent. First and above all, we do not aim at a "perfect" solution in the form of a social process from which all frictions are removed. And this all the less so because we recognized very early that some degree of "disorder" is the precondition for individual self-determination. Nor are we advocating revolutionary measures. It is *order-protecting and order-restoring reform* that is our problem.

THE POSTWAR DISINTEGRATION OF ENGLISH CONFORMITY

Again it is the history of England from which we can obtain some guidance. But now it is its shortcomings rather than its achievements that can teach us a lesson.

As we saw, England's success in reconciling freedom with order was the result of a unique combination of geographical, political, and economic conditions, embedded in a cultural tradition that reached far back into the premodern era. But we also had to realize that many of those propitious circumstances—to mention only its physical isolation, its lead in commercial and industrial capitalism, and the ensuing steady progress of every stratum of its population—withered during the current century. Other seemingly salutary factors—its imperial power and even the conformity of outlook and behavior—proved strangely contradictory in recent times. What on the surface appeared to be forces promoting political stability and neutralizing the threat arising from gross inequality, have since revealed themselves as no more than temporary expedients, unable to cope with new instabilities and a never resolved class conflict.

As a consequence, moderation and the will to compromise—so characteristic of England's liberal era—are giving way to irreconcilable positions on the left and the right. An illusionary call for an antiquated version of socialism struggles against the attempt to put the clock back to the institutional order of the nineteenth century. A nation that half a century ago was still united in pursuing reforms is polarized today by radicals and reactionaries—a schism that conjures up the specter of social unrest, especially if the denunciation of national consensus by the present prime minister foretells the political style of the future.

Thus the sociopolitical structure of contemporary Britain can no longer serve as a paradigm for institutional and attitudinal reform. But its very failings, most of which are shared by the larger nations of the West, point to the kind of transformation that could establish a viable tomorrow: reduction of international tensions, both political and economic; a marked advance toward equity in domestic social and economic relations; an effective substitute for economic growth as understood in the past.

In view of the heavy handicaps that burden the class-ridden larger nations of the West, one may wonder whether the chances for balancing freedom with order are not much more favorable in the smaller nations: the Scandinavian countries, Holland, Switzerland, or even Australia and New Zealand. Some of those nations have a long tradition of freedom, and all of them display a large measure of social and even economic equality. It is there that the welfare state has achieved an amalgamation of private strivings with the public interest.

If this challenge is to mean that the larger nations of the West have much to learn from their smaller neighbors, it is irrefutable. Decentralization, both political and economic, and a far-reaching consensus about basic aspirations have achieved there a degree of social stability that has withstood the impact of considerable transmutations. But all this rests on one foundation: peace and prosperity in the world at large. Their pursuit of reformist goals was, and remains, conditional on their political independence, which in turn is based on a peaceful accommodation among the great powers. What a serious international conflict has in store for the small nations can be read in their fate during World War II. Fear that formal neutrality will no longer offer any security has already induced some of them to seek armed protection under NATO. In a word, their very existence, and thus their paradigmatic significance, is bound up with what the masters of the globe decide.

Thus the locus for initiating the transformation we are speaking of can only be one of the larger nations of the West. Considering the greatly reduced power—military, political, and economic—of all European states, and their apparent inability to form a supranational unit, we cannot expect any of them to take the lead. If at all, it is only in and through the United States that a new, stable order with a satisfactory range of freedom can be initiated.

THE UNITED STATES AS POTENTIAL SUCCESSOR

It is now up to us to discover whether what England represented in the last century the United States can become under the drastically altered conditions of the late twentieth century. To avoid any suspicion that we intend to resurrect the fiction of an "American century," we cannot emphasize too strongly that only *a much transformed* United States can fulfill that mission. But we are also aware that the aims of its present regime, backed by a consenting popular majority, squarely opposes any emancipatory transformation. So we shall have to conduct our inquiry in a spirit of sober realism if not skepticism. If America fails, emancipatory progress as here understood will be foreclosed for any foreseeable time.

No doubt the United States possesses a good many assets that mark it for leadership. Like England in the past, it holds today the preponderant position in the Western world, if not on the globe. In contrast with England then and now, the United States is, together with its regional neighbors, richly endowed with almost all essential resources. If England was the promoter of the first industrial revolution, the United States plays the same, even if not uncontested, role in the present microelectronic revolution. In spite of its plutocratic structure commented on earlier, the United States still enjoys a measure of "classlessness" unparalleled in any of the larger Western countries. It even has its own tradition of spontaneous conformity, though considerably weakened in recent decades.

But there is a reverse side of the medal, a deeply rooted tradition of political and economic individualism that has recurrently rebelled against public intervention and is doing so again. By thus repudiating the main instrument of reform, the success or failure of the United States may depend on whether and in what manner those conflicting traits can be reconciled.

In this respect it is important to remember that until quite recently, the institutional as well as the intellectual history of the country was shaped by a leadership stemming mainly from the eastern part of the country and thus perpetuating an English heritage. In spite of vast differences in the constitutional setup, the foundations of freedom—habeas corpus, Bill of Rights, a steadily expanding franchise—are the same. So was, far into the twentieth century, the preference for societal constraints over political controls.

This institutional and attitudinal affinity of the colonial settlers with the motherland is in many ways surprising, because the setting in which freedom and the forces of societal constraints developed in the New World deviated radically from the experience of the Old. Over all Europe private and public freedom won out after a long struggle with feudalism and absolutism, while the societal constraints were largely a secular residue from the religious bonds of those premodern ages. Contrariwise, in the New World personal freedom marked the very beginning of a new civilization. And societal constraints, at least in the dominant northeast, grew directly out of a living religion, the Puritan creed. Where this source was absent, it was the pressure of an inhospitable environment that enforced its own type of spontaneous conformity upon the settlers.

Ostensibly the motherland retained political control over the colonies. In practice they were from the outset almost independent because communication, not to speak of coercion, was bound to be ineffective over 3,000 miles. The political organization, which the settlers themselves devised, resembled the textbook version of a social contract. Self-government through elected assemblies stood at the cradle of the new nation, even if for a long time confined to a medley of small communities. After all, it took six generations from the landing of the Pilgrim Fathers to the setting up of a federal government with narrowly circumscribed powers. Such a slow and limited growth of centralization not only safeguarded freedom but also fostered the deep sense of social equality that has been a distinctive feature of the average white American, a feeling that is gradually entering into the consciousness of the nonwhite population.

Though it is an important asset for the impending new tasks, *social* equality must not be confounded with *economic* equality. Instead, during almost 400 years of U.S. history, accumulation of landed property, profits from trade in raw materials and slaves, and

the rapid growth of industry supported by mass immigration created a sharp division between rich and poor with all the potentialities of a class struggle in the European fashion. If by and large
such a struggle was avoided, and a spirit of tolerance and individual
independence was preserved, the credit goes to expansion on every
domestic front. Though the "moving frontier" was only one instance, the mere existence of an alternative to factory work favor-
ably affected wages and working conditions in the east—a fact acknowledged even by Marx. At the same time the eastern industrialist
strongly supported the western and, especially, midwestern settler
by presenting him, in Arnold Toynbee's words, with a locomotive
in one hand and a reaper and binder in the other.

Goethe called anyone who promised liberty and equality in the
same breath a fantasist or charlatan. Life on the frontier seems to
refute him, because the rugged individualism of the settlers was
constrained by a kind of protective conformity born in the struggle
with an inhospitable nature and a hostile native population.

No such case can be made for the city dwellers in the new centers of industrialization. There the striking economic inequality would
have choked any spirit of solidarity even if the successive waves of
immigrants had not stemmed from regions with cultural back-
grounds as different from the English stock as from one another.
What the various ethnic groups had in common was not a religious
tradition or mores of daily life. It was a shared dream growing out
of the dreariness of their living and working conditions, and of the
will to overcome this by any means.

Thus, while an unrestrained individualism deeply distrusted
governmental patronage and gave rise to the purest form of laissez-
faire, it also created a unified vision of a better future. In abandon-
ing the traditions of their origins, the second or third generation of
immigrants turned their gaze to a tomorrow of material plenty for
all, and of everyone's fair share in the immaterial treasures that a
free and rich society would accumulate.

More survives of this spirit today than resounds in the com-
plaints about our predicament. But we must be aware that what is
left of the dream is not only a spur but also a curb to appropriate
action. It is a spur because it strengthens the creed that every problem has a good solution. It is a curb when it rejects collective action

as the means to such solutions. But in order fully to understand this ambivalence, we must take our story up to the present.

Three events in the short span of little more than one generation have fundamentally changed the social environment in which the United States developed: the closing of the frontier, the international entanglements beginning with the war with Spain, and the Great Depression. The three events coincided with, and to a large extent promoted, the transition from liberal to *organized capitalism*— a market dominated by the *self-organization of the major producers* but also *progressively subjected to public control*. In fact, the latter was largely a response to the former, first as a protective action against the abuses of private power but, after the Great Depression, with the wider aim of restoring stability to an economic system whose uncontrolled operation assured neither efficiency nor equity of provision.

Both these tendencies went in the direction of collective organization. They were strengthened after World War II through the leading position of the United States in world affairs and its espousal of the welfare state. But its foreign policy thwarted its domestic aspirations. As one of the two superpowers the United States combined an ever more costly "deterrence" with imperialist adventures, while simultaneously pushing social reform toward the vision of the Great Society. Not only did this twofold ambition overtax the nation's resources, it also gradually undermined the consensus that had been established during World War II and maintained during the decades of economic growth.

At first sight the nation seemed to adjust easily to the new sociopolitical framework. But the growing tensions that have afflicted all Western nations—progressive inflation alternating with growing unemployment, rising frictions between rival power groups, and a deepening sense of frustration especially among the young—came to dominate the U.S. scene. What we witness today is a delayed reaction to the profound structural changes that the prosperous postwar decades had masked. It is now evident that wide strata of the middle classes have not made their peace with public controls, nor has an answer been found to the technological challenge.

CONDITIONS OF STABILIZATION

Evading Hot War

On what grounds, then, can one expect the United States to be in a better position to overcome the present predicaments than are its Western partners? Will its assets—world political dominance, vast endowment with resources, technological pioneering, coupled with social classlessness and a conformist vision of the future— suffice to conquer the disruptive forces fed by the heritage of individualism and an instinctive distrust of public controls?

We cannot approach these questions without first forming a concrete notion of what we earlier defined as the minimum conditions for any lasting adjustment to the present stage of emancipation. We shall do so now, always keeping in mind the actual and the potential role that the United States does or should play in such an adjustment.

The first and by far the most important condition is the maintenance of *international peace*. It is the foundation of any advance toward a domestic stabilization that can offer a range for individual self-determination. But it is at the same time the most intractable task of reconstruction. All our worries about domestic disintegration dwindle when we compare it with what we earlier called the latent anarchy in international relations. After all, in the face of economic instability, of blatant inequality, of grave conflicts of group interests, and of ideological discord, all Western nations can still fall back on more elemental links among their citizens, forged by a common language, a common history, and common day-to-day experiences. Even now those factors bestow an astounding stability on the humdrum business of daily life. In a word, the Western nations, though in need of reorganization, are still functioning societies.

Only a creation *ex nihilo* could today establish what can be meaningfully called an international society. But not before the East-West contest and the impetuous claims of the Third World have been assuaged can there evolve even the rudiments of such a society: a feeling of solidarity and, however slow, some institutional convergence. But, and this is the tragic dilemma, those conflicts themselves cannot be assuaged before a spirit of supranational tolerance overcomes nationalist aspirations. While fully aware of the humanitarian achievements—the term taken in its most comprehensive meaning—of many international organizations, we must draw the conclusion that the only effective agents in international politics are still the national states, and ultimately the superpowers. But one might also conclude that in order to lower the temperature, the withdrawal of those powers into their domestic affairs—the apparent aim of the Soviet regime under Gorbachev—might be the safest first step toward peaceful coexistence.

This idea will remain utopian so long as these main protagonists of the latent international civil war conceive of each other as crusaders for world domination. In spite of all protestations to the contrary, the actions of either provide only too many clues for such interpretation. This is no less true of the Asian, African, and Middle-American adventures of the Soviet Union than it is of the avowed intent of the present U.S. government to force on the Soviet regime an arms competition that will exhaust its resources.

Of course, it is impossible to verify what both sides affirm: the purely defensive nature of their military preparations. Still, in view of the undeniable fact that continuation of the arms race is self-defeating, accepting the other power's profession of peaceful intentions while maintaining a military balance may yet imply the least risk for either—on one condition: that *deterrence will be total and equally effective for both powers*.

There we touch on a problem that reveals a twofold inferiority of the West, strategically and psychologically. What is at stake can be best understood in the context of the current debate over whether effective disarmament is feasible before the prevailing political tensions have been reduced and some measure of mutual confidence has been established—or whether such disarmament is itself a precondition for establishing confidence.

In principle I side with the first alternative. But I am aware that it is feasible only after one prior step in the realm of armament has been taken: *the equalization of conventional military forces and their war equipment*. In this realm the West is greatly inferior, an inferiority that is at the root of the installation of new rockets in Europe, and of the West's refusal to renounce a first atomic strike.

This essay goes to press at a highly critical moment. A treaty has been signed about the abolishment of medium range missiles. Moreover, both superpowers have issued emphatic declarations about a worldwide retrenchment of long distance atomic weapons. But unless the United States yields on her program of militarizing space (SDI), the chances for further disarmament, atomic or conventional, are minimal. On the other hand, if a reciprocal reduction of long distance atomic weapons can be arranged after all, equalization of conventional armaments gains in strategic importance.

Therefore, if total deterrence, conventional as well as atomic, is the precondition for shifting the contest of the superpowers to the political plane, and mutual reduction of conventional armaments proves impossible, NATO's conventional defenses must be raised to a level that assures successful resistance to any onslaught. In order to avoid further escalation, such expansion of NATO's arsenal must have a clearly defensive character. But it can be safely combined with the offer of a nonaggression pact and a solemn promise of no first use of atomic weapons.

It is also important to form an estimate of the financial costs of such conventional equalization. Expert opinion has concluded that the additional expenditure would be only a small percentage of the present budget of NATO. The reason is the greater efficiency of the West per unit of man and conventional arms.

I am raising the entire issue not to state an opinion on a matter of high military strategy, for which I am in no way competent. The idea is significant in the context of what I called above a *psychological inferiority* of the West. We can take it for granted that if neither the negotiations in Geneva nor future summit discussions succeed in stopping the arms race, the Soviet people, however grudgingly, will make every sacrifice necessary to keep up the pace. In contrast, public opinion in every Western country has passed over in silence the idea of strengthening conventional deterrence, if it has not outright rejected it, though it was propagated years ago by a representative team of U.S. statesmen with the strong support of the military leaders of NATO. And knowledgeable observers predict that no Western government would stay in power that would dare to submit such a proposal to its parliament.

We meet here with a typical attitude of the man in the street and his political representatives, an attitude we shall encounter again when we examine other preconditions of emancipatory progress:

unwillingness to make small, short-term sacrifices for the safeguarding of long-term interests—in the present case of physical survival. Of course, we must admit that even total deterrence by itself can achieve no more than continuation of a cold peace, perhaps strengthened by more pragmatic responses to particular conflicts. How the split atom, this bitter fruit from the tree of knowledge, can be made politically palatable, no one has so far been able to show.

Toward Productive Regional Autarky

Desirable as it may be that the great powers shift the emphasis of their *political* activity to their domestic affairs, it seems to be a most unlikely step in the prevailing climate of international relations. Perhaps there is a better chance for a retreat behind national or regional boundaries in the field of *economic relations*. Admittedly such a move contradicts conventional wisdom and even the surface of our daily experience. But it may well be in accord with long-term technological tendencies, of which we can already spot some rudiments.

Standard doctrine has it that an essential factor in promoting material welfare is international specialization and exchange, and more than a century of economic development seems to confirm it. But we should be aware that doctrine and experience derive from a peculiar state of affairs: unequal distribution of resources and human skills over the regions of the globe. This datum of the past must not blind us to a fundamental change. Spreading industrialization and the technologies of the atom, of electronics, and of synthetic chemistry are steadily reducing those differences inherited from nature and history. Take as an example the way in which synthetic chemistry offers in more and more fields the ultimate sources of material welfare for use everywhere—by substituting the ubiquitous and unlimited constituents of the inorganic world, the chemical elements, for the localized, scarce products of geological evolution. If in addition atomic fusion and the utilization of solar energy offer an ecologically favorable solution to the problem of power, one can imagine a future in which for most populated regions—the Western Hemisphere, an enlarged European Economic Community and its affiliates, the Warsaw Pact nations, India, and China—*a high degree of technologically sustained autarky* can be accomplished. Contrary to past experience, such autarky could dispense with protection, because it would be far more productive than carrying large amounts of primary and secondary merchandise from and to distant continents. It would be compatible with intensive commerce in specialties, and even with the further internationalization of services, such as communication, banking, and tourism.

No doubt this development will not be consummated during the time span with which we are concerned. We consider it because some relevant beginning is already noticeable: on the one hand, in the *spread of multinational corporations*, and on the other hand, in the *leading position of the service sector* in all mature economies. At first sight the multinationals, by globalizing the influence of national enterprises, seem to strengthen the trend toward internationalization. But, remembering the effect of an earlier imperialism, we can expect that establishing modern industries in less developed regions is bound to promote worldwide decentralization of production in the long run.

Concerning the service sector, which today employs more than half the working population of the West, it is the physical nature of most services—with exceptions as mentioned above—that ties them more closely to domestic demand than is true of commodities.

Thus, far from promoting isolationism, growing regional self-sufficiency seems to be a natural development, with political consequences possibly more favorable to reducing international tensions than the traditional division of labor. We pointed earlier to the one-sided benefits of such division. Even today three-quarters of all earnings from world trade go to the Western 20 percent of the world's population.

We cannot conclude this discussion without pointing to contrary forces that for the time being preclude voluntary dissociation of the national economies. We need only refer to the volume of international debts, the size of capital movements induced by fluctuating interest rates and in turn affecting national trade balances. Along with the budget policy of the United States, misjudgment and pursuit of narrow interests on the part of sectional power groups, such as the banking system of the West and the arms industries, play a dominant role. But overshadowing all those pitfalls is a problem of truly gigantic dimensions—the *development of the Third World*.

It is not ignorance of the facts or insensitivity to mass misery that has so far made me relegate this issue to the background. With everyone else—except the believers in the panacea of private enterprise—I cannot see any solution within the time span with which we are concerned. It has been estimated that at least 300 million men and women are today unemployed in the less developed countries, a pool to which hundreds of millions will be added by the end of the century. Even more generous support on the part of the developed nations, with grants and loans from international agencies, national governments, and private investors, backed by large-scale technical assistance will be only a trickle of what is needed to mobilize latent resources, to supply capital equipment and the implements of an adequate infrastructure, not to mention the improvement of managerial and labor skills and the establishment of an efficient administration.

No doubt vast differences exist among different regions as to the potential for development. Nevertheless, it is not surprising that growing numbers of skeptics among Western observers argue in favor of stopping the entire enterprise. We draw the reverse conclusion by arguing that support should be extended. But we are aware of definite limitations, so long as the West has not found a *modus vivendi* with the world of collectivism that would allow it to devote the bulk of its resources to peaceful purposes at home and abroad.

Equity in Economic and Social Relations

With the international issues left hanging in an uneasy balance, we now turn to our *domestic predicaments*. They extend over the entire latitude of experience: political, socioeconomic, and cultural. All the same, in what follows priority will be given to socioeconomic considerations. We give it not from a belief in the primary relevance of material concerns, but because of a peculiar urgency of those problems, problems that at the same time will prove most amenable to rational solutions. Ultimately our procedure is vindicated by the fact that, perhaps more than ever before, political and cultural forces operate today through socioeconomic institutions and attitudes, converting this sphere into a microcosm of modern life generally.

The first issue to be considered is how to achieve a closer approach to *equity in social and economic relations.* There we now encounter a difficulty that we were spared when discussing international relations and their stabilization. Certainly pursuing that goal
may strain our efforts to the limit, and the means to attain it may
be highly controversial. But there is hardly any controversy about
the nature of the goal itself. In contrast, when striving for more
equity, not only the means but also the ends are the subject of hot
disputes. Who are to be the beneficiaries of a more equitable order?
Labor, as the victim of historical class struggle? Some vaguely defined group called the "poor"? The unorganized strata in contemporary societies who face the new oligarchy of organized capitalism? And what are the benefits to consist of? *Equality of opportunity*
in the struggle for income, wealth, and social status? *Equality of the
results* achieved in that struggle? Moreover, is equity in any form
compatible with the inequality of personal endowments and, if not,
will it not hamper efficiency?

We are not going to restate the arguments for and against those
points of view. In speaking, first of all, about the issue of material
redistribution, we have already refuted the popular myth that the
welfare state has achieved a truly fair distribution of *incomes.* Large
as transfer payments were and still are, they have not prevented
income distribution in the United States from becoming still more
unequal. And if the clamor for a further reduction of those payments should succeed, we shall be in for an era of growing inequality. Were we to include in our observation the distribution of *wealth—*
it has been estimated that in the United States 1 percent of
Americans own at least one-quarter of all private wealth—the plutocratic nature of the social order, perpetuated by the laws of in-
heritance, would be beyond dispute.

For the purpose of reform it is necessary to break down those
global figures. Then the major victims of maldistribution of incomes are women, certain ethnic groups, and, above all, the young.
Again, in the United States men are 17 times as likely to hold top
jobs as are women, and whites are 7 times as likely to hold such
jobs as are blacks. Moreover, average earnings of women are still
only 60 percent of what men earn, irrespective of the level of performance. On the other hand, 50 percent of all those who are un-

employed, and thus deprived of earning power, are concentrated among those who are 16 to 24 years old.

These facts destroy another myth. All Western societies pride themselves on having abolished the privilege of status and other open discrimination by offering all their citizens *equality of opportunity*. Does this not enable every person to attain an economic and social position in accord with his or her abilities and efforts?

It stands to reason that opportunities are equal only if the starting conditions in the competitive race are more or less the same. Let us face the fact that this proviso amounts to a total obliteration of history and of the barriers it has erected over centuries if not millennia. We also begin to understand that the main victims of inequality of opportunity are not individuals chosen at random, but specific *groups*—sexual and ethnic—from which no individual can escape. To these groups we must, of course, add the less homogeneous stratum that the British call the "working classes." Originally fed by quite divergent sources—dispossessed agrarian populations, displaced craftsmen, poor immigrants, and other victims of capitalist evolution—today they form the equivalent of a class. Neither equal human rights nor free access to bargaining, and lately to education, has so far eradicated their inferiority as judged by the standards of the marketplace.

It is a growing realization of these barriers that has led to the demand to supplement equality of opportunity with public measures assuring *equality of outcome*. In other words, the verdict of the market is to be corrected by administrative decision. An example would be planned reduction of the gap between the after-tax incomes of the well-paid and the poorly paid. That such measures need not be confined to the economic realm is shown by quotas for minorities in admission to higher education or the demand for universal health insurance covered by public funds.

However, even those who deem such a reform fair must admit that greater equity achieved by political *fiat* may provoke a *conflict between equity and efficiency*. Were such a policy adopted internationally, so as not to affect the competitive strength of an individual nation in the world market, one might argue that by now the mature countries are rich enough to decide the conflict in favor of equity. Otherwise, only lasting technological superiority would make it a viable reform for a particular nation—a rather unrealistic "beggar my neighbor" policy, considering the rapid dispersion of innovations. Moreover, as we shall presently see, the ongoing technological revolution is more likely to reinforce inequality.

But there is an obstacle to planned equalization that goes beyond considerations of efficiency. Equalization in any form is advocated as a means of strengthening the spirit of spontaneous conformity on the part of the hitherto underprivileged. But the negative reaction to egalitarian policies all over the West demonstrates that inequality is deeply imbedded in Western culture, and public controls designed to overcome it seem to preclude the very consensus for the sake of which they are advocated.

Thus, realistically we must reckon with a lengthy transition during which the historical barriers can be gradually lowered. Even such incremental progress will be achieved only if gainers and losers alike recognize that sociopolitical stabilization must have priority over radical abolition of privileges, and is a prerequisite for it.

Planned Domestic Colonization

We saw earlier that during the liberal era, and even during the early stages of organized capitalism, the demand for redistribution was muted because steady growth of output assured all strata a rising standard of living. In retrospect one may regret that some redistribution was not then initiated by reapportioning the gains from growth. Today the multiple impediments to economic expansion of the former style, which we discussed, preclude such an evasive solution. For this reason it is of paramount importance to search for a *substitute for the growth mechanisms of the past*.

There is indeed an alternative, which can be defined as *planned domestic colonization*. The very term is a challenge. It suggests that even the mature regions of the West are not fully "developed," and are in need of collective action in order to consummate their latent potentialities.

Characteristic symptoms of such "immaturity" are a one-sided emphasis on material goods for individual use and a lack of social overhead capital, the so-called infrastructure. To be specific, most Western societies are undersupplied with nonmaterial provisions, such as education, health care, and other social services, not to speak of everything that belongs to the dimension of aesthetics and general culture. Yet inadequate supply extends, especially in the United States, even to the material substructure without which the ordinary functions of production and consumption cannot be performed—from road building and water supply, slum clearing and the other items of urban renewal, and reorganization and extension of public transportation, to a solution of the energy problem that is compatible with environmental protection, to mention some of the most urgent needs.

Most of these items bear the character of *public goods and services*. They are *indivisible*, in that their benefits accrue to society at large, like national defense, fire protection, and highways. They cannot be bought or even used by any individual independent of their use by others, as is the case with ordinary private goods, such as food and clothing. Nor is there any practical way of *measuring the benefit* that public goods bestow on an individual.

Those characteristics preclude most of those goods and services from being channeled through the market. And though some of them can in principle be produced and sold on an individual basis, the market is unlikely to provide them in satisfactory quantity and quality at acceptable prices—education is the outstanding example. This is because, high as their social value is when judged by cultural standards, few if any of those goods and services are profitable in terms of private enterprise. They are the natural objects of provision through public agencies, to be financed by saving on current public expenditures or (and) by transfer of purchasing power from the private domain.

There is, of course, a limit to such domestic colonization, set by the magnitude of resources required to satisfy the ordinary needs of society. But one might well argue that all Western societies today have excess resources at their disposal that would go a long way toward raising the cultural level, if they were not diverted by a taste structure shaped by advertising and contrary standards of the media. Still, considering the psychological obstacles that stand in the way of altering tastes—not to forget that there may be justifiable disagreements in a domain so highly laden with "values"—the latest emancipatory breakthrough in the shape of a technological revolution may help us to succeed in "colonizing" without restricting the range of prevailing provision.

Whatever the ultimate verdict will be on the approaching "computer society," there can be no doubt about its high level of productivity. Not only will this help domestic colonization to open the gates to a new area of welfare, but the rising demand for resources and, in particular labor resources, can serve as an effective antidote to the *peril* inherent in the same *technology-growing, long-lasting unemployment*.

As was indicated earlier, this issue was masked so long as inflation appeared as the main threat. It was still blurred during the phase of planned deflation, which was an independent source of mass unemployment. It has come into the open in the present recovery when a hard core of unemployed—of a magnitude formerly experienced only at the bottom of depressions—has not been affected by reflationary measures of fiscal and monetary control, and certainly to the forces of a free market. Nor is the redefinition of full employment as equal to 6-7 percent unemployment, as some "experts" have proposed, a practical solution.

Because it is mainly events in the economic realm that, besides the hazards in international politics, block the advance toward the emancipatory goal, our next task will be a study of those negative effects of the new technology, and the attempt to devise a policy suitable to overcome them. By opening new employment opportunities, domestic colonization can, in principle, turn what at first sight appears as a major failing of the new technology into a veritable boon. I say "in principle" because, in the prevailing public opinion of the West, we shall encounter grave obstacles to taking the necessary steps.

6 The Specter of Technological Unemployment

SOURCES OF LONG-TERM UNEMPLOYMENT: THE NEW TECHNOLOGY

It will be instructive to recapitulate as an introduction what we said earlier about the size and composition of present-day unemployment. We then distinguished between a *quasi-cyclical* and a *structural phenomenon*. Most conspicuous in recent experience and the primary target of policy were the millions of workers of every category who lost their jobs as a consequence of planned deflation. Though different in origin from the anonymous forces that caused a cyclical downswing in the past, the symptoms of falling output and falling employment all around were similar enough to suggest, even if under a different label, the use of the conventional antidepression measures: tax reduction and public works (the latter in the United States in the form of large-scale rearmament). Indeed, wherever it was adopted, this policy proved successful, the United States cutting the top rate of unemployment to roughly one-half.

What was, however, quite untypical was the magnitude of unemployment that persisted during the subsequent revival and still persists. Evidently there are factors at work, quite different from planned deflation, that are dislocating a sizeable part of the labor force. For this type of unemployment the label "structural" is quite appropriate, because it is the consequence of a lasting change in the basic structure of the market, a change that we trace back to a *technological revolution*.

In order to penetrate to the core of the problem, we must distinguish between two different modes in which technological change today affects the labor market, especially in the United States. There are, first of all, the so-called *sunset industries*, of which steel, textiles, ship building, and nowadays machine tools are typical examples. These industries have recently been losing out to technologically superior competitors from other countries—developed and even less developed ones—and this not only in the world market but even in the domestic field. Second, we are faced with shrinking employment opportunities in the most productive enterprises, which avail themselves of the new technology of *automation*.

It may be objected that neither of these experiences is really novel. We need only to remember the plight of the British textile industry during the interwar period, caused by the industrialization of some of its former export regions. The plight was overcome partly by reorganization, partly by the so-called south migration, which moved large sections of former textile workers into new, more modern fields of production. No doubt the predicament of today's sunset industries can be overcome in a similar manner—by technological improvement and also by the transfer of capital and labor to *"sunrise"* industries, among them especially the rapidly developing information sector. In either case adjustment will be facilitated by clear price signals indicating the locus of new profit opportunities.

The situation is radically different when we now turn to the unemployment problem that the *microelectronic revolution* poses. Again it is widely held that the problem is not new. And it is true that over the last 200 years the capitalist labor markets have been periodically exposed to technological shocks, shocks that were absorbed, even if sometimes with a considerable time lag, by the uncontrolled forces of private consumption and investment. So the problem boils down to the question of whether the employment effect of the new technology differs basically from those earlier impacts.

In order to understand that this is really so, we must examine the mechanism that compensated for technological unemployment in the past. In a nutshell, it was the *overall growth of the capitalist system* that offered almost unlimited employment opportunities over the long run. To be specific, we must note that the technologically displaced were hardly ever taken back into their former occupations. They shifted, first, from the originally dominant agrarian sector to the expanding sector of mining, manufacture, and construction, and within this sector from the standard consumption and investment industries—textile and steel—to chemical and electrotechnical production. The process culminated in the mass movement of workers into the labor-intensive part of the service sector, in particular into trade, finance, and professional and administrative services, both private and public. With the predominance of office work these occupations have become the main receptacles of surplus labor during the course of the present century.

What is truly revolutionary about the new technology is its impact on this tertiary sector. Automation is no longer confined to goods production, substituting machinery for human muscle. On an ever larger scale it is about to take over all mental functions that can be routinized, including the lower echelons of management. In this way it is bound in the long run to transform the former receptacles into new sources of unemployment.

If it was the steady growth of the capitalist system that neutralized the distortions in the labor market, this safety valve is, as we saw earlier, rapidly closing. International tensions, political unrest in the Third World aggravated by trade barriers, and the ecological limitations discussed above progressively block the former trend. Industrialization of less developed countries transfers employment opportunities to those regions, and enables them to compete successfully in the markets of the mature countries. This is the global environment in which the West must, from now on, achieve compensation for technological unemployment.

WHY AN UNCONTROLLED MARKET CANNOT COMPENSATE FOR THE DISPLACEMENT EFFECT OF THE NEW TECHNOLOGY

The obstacles that this environment places in the path toward a satisfactory employment level in the mature countries are quite serious. But the core of the problem lies within those countries themselves, in the response of the strategic domestic forces, especially of potential investors, to the impact of the new technology. This response is the ultimate test of whether we are confronted with a novel threat to the system's stability, or whether such fears are as unwarranted as were the anxieties of the Luddites in the early nineteenth century. The latter, optimistic view is still dominant not only among businessmen but also among professional experts. For this reason a careful analysis of the related issues cannot be omitted. If such an analysis is to persuade the professional reader—and without his or her support there is little hope that the necessary political consequences will result—the following exposition cannot help bearing a somewhat technical character. But my main propositions appeal to mere common sense and should offer an overall view of the matter also to the general reader.

To approach the problem we must, first of all, distinguish between two categories of innovations: *process innovations*, which offer "new ways of making old things," and *product innovations*, using "old or new ways for making novel things." A modern example of the first category is a robot's substituting for human activity the mechanical motions of an electronically steered instrument. The best-known examples of the second category are the railroads, the telephone, and, above all, the automobile.

In principle either category tends to displace labor. But it is a frequent feature of product innovations to create secondary effects that on balance render them labor-attracting. The most often cited example is the linkages of automobile production with the expansion of the rubber industry, the building of gas stations, and, above all, the construction of a vast highway system. Though one must not unduly generalize this experience—the cases are too numerous in which the public rejected a novelty, creating a waste of resources, including labor—it is a fair presumption that labor displacement, and thus its compensation, are primarily problems associated with *process innovations*.

We have so far spoken only of those process innovations whose primary effect is a reduction of labor input. What about *capital-saving* innovations? Their importance must certainly not be underrated; we need only to think of the process of miniaturization, which has resulted in the microcomputer.

It is true that *applying* a reduced capital stock as a means of innovation may or may not be accompanied by a simultaneous reduction of labor input. Even when it is not, we must take into account what happens while the new capital stock is itself produced, that is, the employment situation in the *capital-producing industries*. Innovations that cheapen their output, which is what "capital-saving" amounts to, is as a rule accompanied by a reduction of labor input, so that in this indirect manner capital-saving innovations also pose a compensation problem.

We can now formulate more precisely what the real issue is. No serious student will deny that process innovations, and especially those of the microelectronic type, displace labor. Nor would he or she deny that, in principle, compensation is possible. What is in dispute is the question of whether the market system of late capitalism is endowed with a *self-regulating mechanism* capable of achieving compensation by the uncontrolled actions of private consumers and producers, or whether *public intervention* is necessary in order to counter destabilizing tendencies that an uncontrolled market is likely to create.

The believers in the compensatory effectivenenss of a free market derive their faith from a few arguments that, if they had any validity in the past, have lost it in the new technological environment. The first one is often presented in the absurd formulation according to which the displaced will find reemployment in building the capital stock that displaces them. To make some sense of the idea, we might assume that some of the workers displaced by an earlier innovation have not yet been reabsorbed when the next innovation comes along, and are thus available for its introduction. Even so, if the second innovation is to be profitable—the prime condition for its introduction—the quantity of labor thus reemployed must be smaller or cheaper than the labor it displaces.

The main trust in the compensating power of a free market is grounded in the proposition that process innovations *increase aggregate demand*. After all, such an innovation reduces unit costs of the innovated output, thus creating a surplus in the hands of the innovator so long as prices can be kept above costs. And even when the innovation has been dispersed and prices fall, an equivalent surplus accrues to the buyers of the innovated output in the form of an increase in their real purchasing power. When either of those surpluses is applied as demand for goods or services, will this not provide automatic compensation?

Alas, what the argument overlooks is the harsh fact that the dis

placed have not only lost their working places but also their previous income, which eliminates their prior demand for wage goods.
In other words, simultaneously with the surplus in purchasing power
an equivalent deficit has occurred, threatening to displace additional workers in the wage-goods industries. The only way to avoid
this is the substitution of the demand of the surplus recipients for
the lost demand of the displaced. In this way a balancing economic
circuit can be restored—from which, however, the displaced remain eliminated.[1]

So far we have unduly simplified our presentation by assuming
that the innovator keeps output and sales price at the original level.
It may pay him to reduce the price of the innovated output if by
doing so he can raise sales more than proportionately. In that case
fewer workers—ideally none at all—will be displaced from the innovating enterprise. But this procedure by no means cancels the
displacement effect altogether. The additional demand now di-
rected toward the innovated output must be withdrawn from other
producers, creating displacement in those firms.

It is unlikely that the innovator can maintain a quasi-monopolis-
tic position for long. New entrants will imitate the innovation, raising the aggregate of innovated output and thus reducing its price.
This will certainly be a boon to general welfare, but will this process of *dispersion* not also achieve compensation? Participants in dispersion must, first of all, build a new capital stock, an investment
that attracts labor. Is this, then, the self-regulating mechanism
through which autonomous market forces reabsorb the originally
displaced?

Alas, this possibility will be annulled by two countervailing factors. Employment of the new capital stock will not increase, but
only *shift*, the demand for labor. There is indeed an increase in
such demand while the new stock is being *built*. From then on,
however, labor input falls back to what is required for steady replacement of the new capital stock. This input will exceed the prior
employment for this purpose only if such replacement is more labor-intensive—a highly unlikely case, given the new technology.

But even if replacement were to require more labor, this compensating effect would be more than canceled out by the consequences of the *application* of the new stock. It was built as a labor-
saving device with the prospect of a surplus. But such a surplus

arises only if the *operation* of the stock *displaces more labor* than must be added for *replacement*. In a word, rather than acting as a force of compensation, *dispersion adds to the pool of the displaced*.

Our conclusion must be that neither consumption of the surplus nor dispersion of the innovation will serve to reabsorb the displaced. The reason is that reabsorption is conditional on the *creation of new working places*, to be provided *by the formation of new real capital*. The argument was only partially valid so long as "pure" services had a large share in overall provision. It must be generalized under the new technological regime in which real capital plays an increasing role in the service sector, if personal services are not altogether reduced to a kind of disguised unemployment, as Lord Kaldor recently pointed out.

If it could be shown that investment of the innovational surplus was an *automatic* response to the presence of a large pool of unemployed, the "optimists" might still carry the day. But the investment path is beset by impediments too strong for it to be pursued by prudent decision makers.

First of all, there is a deterrent in the form of a *time problem*. Building a capital *stock* requires the investment of surplus *flows* extending over a long period, during which displacement persists, dashing investors' profit expectations and inducing them to hoard available funds.

Furthermore, pessimistic expectations will be fed by *special risks* that are inseparable from this type of investment. We can pinpoint them with the help of the conventional distinction between induced and spontaneous investment. We speak of *induced* investment as the response of an investor to a rise in demand that cannot be met with the available productive capacity, and thus requires expansion of the capital stock. There is no uncertainty about the direction such expansion is to take. An unambiguous signal—a rise in price—indicates the nature of the goods additionally demanded, at the same time assuring the investor of the profitability of such investment.

The free market offers no such guidance in the case of *spontaneous* investment required for compensation of technological unemployment. There is no prior price signal that would indicate the quality or quantity of future demand. If undertaken at all, such investment must base itself on the *uncertain expectation* that once the new capital stock is available, its output will find a fitting demand—a demand that is itself created by the remuneration of the factors of production that spontaneous investment is to put into employment.

But perhaps the strongest impediment countering spontaneous investment is one frequently discussed in the context of a "takeoff into economic development." There it is generally admitted that investment will be undertaken only if any one such act is accompanied by several others. Only then can an individual investor expect that sufficient demand will be forthcoming for his or her future output, because a number of "batches" of factors, each employed in one firm, can become customers for all the others. In other words, the profitability of any one investment depends on *solidary action* by a number of investors. But where can one find in an uncontrolled market a "self-regulating mechanism" that would establish such solidarity and with it a new balancing circuit of transactions?[2]

But have I not left out of consideration a labor-attracting factor that I earlier stressed, *product innovations*? Remember, however, my warning against a rash generalization of the experience with the automobile and its many "linkages." At any rate, the microelectronic novelties that reached the market for consumer goods—small calculators, digital watches, video games and other items of the entertainment industry—have not proved job-creating on a large scale. Obviously one cannot foresee, and for this reason should not discount, future developments. But it would be the height of irresponsibility were we to face the threats to stability that modern process innovations pose in the spirit of Mr. Micawber that "something will turn up."

What has so far turned up is a wave of mergers, that is, gargantuan conglomerates of existing working places, but few new ones.

The rationale of this development is only rarely understood. It is a riskless alternative to spontaneous investment—the true measure of compensating technological unemployment.

Instead, we should not overlook another destructive tendency to which the present state of the labor market points: growing *inequality of status and level of performance*. The psychological and social consequences of large-scale, long-lasting, if not permanent, unemployment need not be elaborated; they conjure up the specter of the "two nations" of which Disraeli spoke as a result of the first industrial revolution. But even for the majority of the employed, a drastic change in the quality of the available jobs is about to create a new stratification, hardly less divisive than the traditional class structure.

It is in the nature of the new technology to expand the opportunity for high-quality work, but the relatively small size of those occupations limits their absorptive capacity. For the vast majority a radical change in the "tier structure" of occupations amounts to a devaluation of skill and a fall in remuneration. To be specific, the former three-tier structure—high, medium, and low quality of work—is being replaced by a two-tier structure, from which the medium quality—craftsmen and clerical personnel—is progressively eliminated. The fact that a growing segment of the shrinking tier will be women creates a special problem. It seems to lead to their competing for low-quality jobs formerly held by men. The steepening of the income pyramid, which is one result of these changes, has made some observers wonder whether the plenty of goods and services that the new technology promises can be distributed through the market at all.

PALLIATIVE MEASURES OF COMPENSATION

Only in passing we mention some *palliative measures* intended to raise the level of employment: extension of part-time work, abolition of overtime, early retirement, promotion of versatile training and retraining as preparation for occupational shifts. We also must not forget an alternative popular in some segments of the counterculture, withdrawal from society at large into a rather nebulous autarky. We do not waste time evaluating the efficiency of those measures, because they are based on a conviction we do not share: that the negative effects on employment of the new technology are inseparable from its benefits, so that all we can do is find makeshift receptacles for the victims.

This ultimately is also true of the most heatedly debated project—an overall reduction of individual working hours, the vacancies thus created to be filled from the ranks of the unemployed. Ignoring some organizational complications and also acknowledging the limited effectiveness of such an arrangement, no valid objections can be raised so long as wages are reduced in proportion to the reduction of working hours. Such an adjustment is, however, hotly contested, and understandably so, by the representatives of organized labor. Only an increase in aggregate purchasing power, they insist, comprising the unchanged wage income of the presently employed plus the increment accruing to those who would occupy the vacancies thus created, could provide the stimulus for a resumption of growth. Moreover, they contend that such a policy would only continue the trend of the last 150 years.

As a counterargument the employers point to the rise in unit costs of such an arrangement, which would compel them to raise prices, with adverse effects on exports and the danger of reactivating a wage-price spiral that would rekindle inflation. Another response to the union demands is the proposal to extend the work week, and thus aggregate output, a procedure that might balance rising direct costs with the fall of overhead costs per unit of output.

Generally speaking, it is true that, in the course of capitalist evolution, the average work week has gradually been reduced from more than 80 to less than 40 hours. But this did not happen as a means of providing working places for the unemployed. On the contrary, to keep production costs down, employers availed themselves of labor-saving innovations, and they might well do so again today. The real effect of the measure would then be the contrary of what labor expects—a further filling rather than a draining of the pool of the long-term unemployed.

The situation would be different if, following a reduction of working time, employers would continue paying only for the hours worked, the loss of earned income on the part of the workers being compensated by a special fund financed by taxation. In this way aggregate workers' income would be made up of an earned and a social income, irrespective of the length of the working day or the number of days worked per week. The details of such a scheme have been set out in an interesting paper by André Gorz (Lettres Internationale, Spring 1986). It stands to reason that such an arrangement requires institutional changes that go far beyond the range of reform considered in this essay.

Surveying the total complex of problems that technological unemployment poses and is likely to magnify in the future, one might well be tempted to advocate a policy that would prolong the experience of the last 30 years by reducing the speed of dispersion of the new technology. The former block—the high cost of the necessary hardware—is practically eliminated by the miniaturization of the equipment. But a substitute could be found by declaring technological unemployment a "diseconomy." Any automating enterprise might be charged with maintaining the workers it displaces until they have found new jobs. Such an imputation of the social costs of innovating to the private beneficiaries would yield a profit only to innovations of very high productivity, reducing dispersion to a trickle. In the highly unlikely case of international application, such a policy might be effective. In a single nation it could succeed only when combined with a strict control of capital movements and a wall of protective tariffs.

While thinking about ways and means to escape the dismal effects of the new technology, it seems only fair to point in passing to an unplanned development that may remove the issue of long-term technological unemployment once and for all from the agenda of future generations. I am speaking of a *demographic change* that will radically alter the conditions in capitalist labor markets, though its consummate effect will be felt at a time that lies far beyond the span with which this essay is concerned.

Assuming that the prevailing low fertility rates will continue, the Western populations will, by the middle of the next century, be radically transformed. On the one hand, they will approach a stationary level, if they have not already fallen. On the other hand, and more important in the present context, their age composition will have drastically changed—a major shift from the young to the old.

Though to some extent this will be true of all Western nations, what is at stake will be most strikingly demonstrated in an extreme example—the changing age composition in the Federal Republic of Germany. At present, in a total population of about 58 million, the age group of 60 years and above comprises roughly 20 percent of the total. By the year 2000 its share is estimated at 30 percent and is expected to rise to 40 percent by the year 2030. A major factor in this development, besides the low birth rates, is the steadily rising life expectancy. In the past, rising longevity has stimulated the participation of the aged in the work process to only a minor degree, a reluctance that is unlikely to change. So we must conclude that 50 years hence, in a total population estimated at 41 million, less than 50 percent of this total, compared with more than 60 percent at present, will have to provide the economic sustenance for all—roughly comprising the age groups from 18 to 60 years of age.

It stands to reason that under such conditions a satisfactory provision of the population is conditional on a level of productivity that only the widest dispersion of automation can guarantee. The consequent reduction of labor input per unit of output—a true "saving of labor"—will no longer obstruct maximum employment.

It would be a grave fallacy to conclude that such a development would automatically establish social harmony and conformity of outlook. The difference in taste structure between young and old will require a major change in the structure of production, while the present system of financing Social Security will prove incompatible with the steady rise of total claims. The foremost danger will be a new division of the Western societies into two hostile camps—this time a struggle of generations in which the young and middle-aged will refuse to carry a load that the aged claim as a fundamental human right.

PLANNED DOMESTIC COLONIZATION AS A POLICY OF COMPENSATION

The time has come for criticism to yield to an attempt to solve our problem. In fact, the core of a solution is implied in the criticism itself. If today no self-regulating mechanism exists to which compensation of technological unemployment can be entrusted, successful adjustment must rely on *public intervention*. Once this principle is accepted, a number of control procedures offer themselves. What will be proposed here is in line with the dual structure of late capitalism: the linkage of a private domain with a public domain. A primary role falls to the openings for employment that can be provided through what we termed planned domestic colonization.

Our scheme tries to safeguard the integrity of the private domain as the main vehicle of the new technology, while extending and reinforcing the scope of the public domain through strengthening of the infrastructure and the provision of largely nonmaterial services hitherto neglected. What we propose is neither revolutionary nor even original. Comparable models have been promulgated under the heading of a guaranteed job program in scholarly treatises, public magazines, and even legislative proposals, such as the Humphrey-Hawkins Bill, proposals of which "For Further Reading" offers some examples. What perhaps gives our scheme an edge is its concern with the specific obstacles that obstruct compensation in a laissez-faire system: the need for formation of real capital and the uncertainties that surround spontaneous investment decisions.

Unlike private investors, public investors—the legislators of the body politic and their executive agents—are not hampered by uncertainties about future demand, because they themselves determine the purpose that investment and its final output is to serve, for instance, the items that make up the infrastructure. Independent of the preferences ruling in the private domain, they are guided by notions of public utility as determined by political decision. For the same reason there is no need to equate outlays with receipts; what in the private domain would be an irretrievable loss can always be balanced with collective revenue.

Nor does the public controller have to confine himself or herself to goods production dependent on prior construction of real capital. A vast array of more or less *pure services* in the fields of health, education, and general welfare is at his or her disposal, restoring the service sector as a receptacle for labor. What supplies are thus mobilized by public control are in the main *labor-intensive*. To the extent to which the computer gains entrance into those services, its role seems to be complementary rather than competitive with labor, with education as a good example. In reorganizing the infrastructure it may even prove socially advantageous to forgo automation and preserve a labor-intensive technology—an alternative that the competitive nature of the private domain excludes.

Many of the new jobs in the infrastructure are especially suited for the absorption of blue-collar workers. However, special provision is necessary for the bulk of white-collar workers whom the automation of the office will gradually displace. To them the expanding range of welfare services offers new opportunities.

It is no minor consideration that a shift of employment to labor-intensive activities and, especially, to more or less pure services is also an *ecological windfall*. These activities claim a minimum of scarce natural resources, and they do not pollute the environment.

What is the *order of magnitude of working places* thus created relative to the likely demand? At this early stage the answer can only be speculative. Some indication is given in an estimate by Prof. Walt W. Rostow, according to which the backlog in the U.S. infrastructure in need of overhauling amounts to between $2 and $3 trillion. As not only the nature but also the size and speed of transformation is a political decision, it can easily be adapted to any changes in the size of the idle labor force, always considering the costs involved.

This now raises a question that, from the outset, may have been in the reader's mind: *how to finance such a scheme*. In answering it I start from the legal and moral obligation on the part of contemporary governments to maintain the unemployed at a decent level of subsistence. From this I conclude that the savings from an otherwise inescapable public expenditure on unemployment compensation will go a long way toward defraying the costs of such a scheme.

In order to offer some numerical backing to this claim, I refer to an unpublished study by Prof. Philip Harvey, in which he estimates the labor costs that would have arisen if the involuntarily unemployed at the depth of the latest recession had been employed in the public domain at going wages. Comparing those costs with the sums actually spent on maintaining them in idleness, he concludes that about 75 percent of the potential employment costs could have been financed from the actual unemployment benefits, leaving a deficit of about $35 billion.

This outcome needs to be qualified if used in our context. The deficit would be raised by additional capital expenditures arising especially in overhauling the infrastructure. But it should also be reduced by at least one-third, because the above calculation refers to a total of more than 12 million unemployed. It includes not only the technologically unemployed but also the victims of the planned deflation, whose reemployment can, and actually has been, successfully entrusted to a fiscal and monetary policy of reflation. Setting off the two items against each other, we can reduce the remaining deficit to about 10 percent of the current budget for military defense. And remember that expenditure on creating maximum employment has a good deal in common with military defense. It will buy not only additional welfare but also a main weapon with which to uphold domestic peace.

With further dispersion of the new technology, the number of claimants is likely to rise, and with it the deficit. But even disregarding the absorption that demography will gradually provide, there is an absolute limit to the number of workers the private domain can dispense with, and thus an automatic limit to the auxiliary support of the public domain.

We have not mentioned the innovational surpluses as a further source of finance. Certainly equity demands that those funds be taxed, but at a rate that will not discourage innovation. Rather, such taxation might be used as a means of controlling the speed of dispersion. What ultimately assures the success of such a scheme is the *climate of prosperity* in which it will operate, with a rise in productivity that steadily raises real incomes and thus strengthens the taxable capacity of the entire population.

OBSTACLES TO PUBLIC INTERVENTION

So it seems that we can conclude our survey of the essential conditions for pursuit of the emancipatory path in a hopeful mood. Maintenance of peace, broader equity, and the "taming" of the new technology are within the range of the possible, and this without any revolutionary breakup of existing sociopolitical structures. Even what may at first appear as a novel factor—the extension of the public domain and its influence on the course of the macroprocess—fits well into the trend of the last half-century. This can be easily demonstrated by a few figures that reveal the present weight of the public domain in our "mixed" system.

More than one-third of the labor force employed today in the United States receives its income from public funds. Were we to add their dependents and also the recipients of transfer payments with their families, the share would rise to half of the population. Of even greater significance may be the fact that half of all the jobs created during the last generation owe their existence to the same source.

And yet we must beware of rash optimism. So far our analysis has been instrumental, that is, we have studied institutional and attitudinal changes to the extent to which they are *suitable means* for moving the system toward the stipulated goal. But we must not overlook the deep gap that separates the *actual* attitudes that today rule the sociopolitical process from the *suitable* ones. At the same time, we have recognized again and again that it is those attitudes which are the strategic factor in any transformation, without the proper performance of which the most perfect blueprints of new institutions remain just that.

The reasons for this discrepancy are manifold. Perhaps the strongest factor is the power structure of late capitalism, typified by the military-industrial complex, the multinational corporations, and other special-interest groups. But we should not underrate another factor peculiar to U.S. tradition and swaying the outlook of ordinary men and women—the profound distrust of collective action, which denies legitimacy to the public domain. The best example is the attitude toward taxation, which is still widely seen as a sacrifice of authentic private consumption and investment in favor of a "public household" with unproductive aims.

There was some truth in this conception when absolutist regimes squandered scarce resources on a sybaritic court life or on military adventures. That today the linkage between taxation and public expenditure is just another mechanism with which we buy external and internal security, and the vast array of public goods and services that the market cannot or will not deliver, has not yet entered conventional wisdom.

Resistance to some of our proposals may be further increased by the current use of taxation for redistribution in the form of transfer payments. But we are not asking the "rich" to sustain the "poor." What we advocate is a type of investment that will enlist millions of job-seeking workers, whom the private domain cannot employ, in productive activity. This is only one, though perhaps the most glaring, example in which social reintegration is thwarted by goal-inadequate behavior. Whether this, too, can be changed, and by what means, is a question that now moves to the center of our inquiry.

NOTES

1. One might object that under the rules of the welfare state, the threat to the wage-goods industries is mitigated by the extent to which the displaced receive unemployment compensation. Correct as a statement of fact, for the believers in a self-regulating market mechanism this is hardly a legitimate argument.

2. Considering all these obstacles to spontaneous capital formation in a

free market, it is quite understandable that, since the days of John Bates Clark a century ago, the "optimists" have been searching for a way of providing additional working places *without the formation of a new capital stock*. Some professional readers may wonder why this "solution" has been passed over in the text.

The answer is that however we judge the abstract logic of those propositions, their practical significance in the world of industrial capitalism is very limited. I am referring, first of all, to the *marginal productivity theorem*, according to which, in principle, any quantity of labor can be combined with a given quantity of fixed capital, provided only that wages adjust to the changing productivity of labor—in the case under consideration, downward. Now remember that the capital stocks we are dealing with are "frozen" in a specific form appropriate to the production of a specific output. It may yet be possible to add, say, in traditional farming or retail trade a small quantity of labor to the already operating crew. In industry, however, the situation is radically different, irrespective of any wage level. For purely physical-technical reasons, adding another worker to the number of workers operating, say, a loom or a Linotype machine is likely to bring the total productivity of labor to zero and below.

Another, more realistic alternative to capital formation is the introduction of *more than one shift*. For a fixed number of displaced this may indeed offer a solution. But under present and forthcoming conditions of an overall technological transformation, displacement will be a continuing process, rapidly raising user costs and setting a definite limit to the expansion of employment by several shifts.

It is on the basis of these deliberations that I conclude that, after the practical elimination of marketable pure services, capital formation is a prime condition for compensation.

Behavior in the Private Domain:
The True Private Interest

In pondering the ways and means of transforming behavior, we confront the crucial problem of this investigation. But before starting on it, we must guard against a misunderstanding of our intent. Transforming behavior, as here understood, is no attempt at substituting for the individual self and its strivings men and women who are exclusively inspired by a spirit of altruism and totally devoted to societal concerns. In other words, we do not envisage a "new personality," but appeal to the old Adam and Eve with interests of their own and the will to pursue them.

When thus studying behavior we have to deal with two categories of actors: the individuals and groups who compose the *private domain*—the topic of the present chapter—and the representatives of the *public domain* who guard, control, and in some measure even replace the members of the private domain. In the latter category, to be discussed in the next chapter, we shall include the heads of major private organizations, with the managers of large corporations as a typical example. The scope of their controlling power and responsibility places them side by side with the public agents.

WELFARE STATE AND WELFARE SOCIETY

I know no better way of coming to the essential point than by quoting from Prof. William Robson's study *Welfare State and Welfare Society*. There our domestic failures are traced to the vain attempt at *building a welfare state without at the same time building a welfare society*. Let me quote some of his axiomatic propositions:

> The welfare state is what . . . government does. The welfare society is what people do, feel, and think about matters of general welfare. . . . Unless people generally reflect the policies and assumptions of the welfare state in their attitudes and actions, it is impossible to fulfill the objectives of the welfare state. . . . When an industrial nation becomes a welfare state the need for a strong sense of individual, group and institutional responsibility and the need for social discipline becomes [*sic*] far greater. . . . (pp. 7, 11)

We can easily apply the terms "welfare state" and "welfare society" as there defined to our reform program, with the result that Robson's and our views fully coincide. What for him is a commitment of people to attitudes and actions that reflect the policies and assumptions of the welfare state—the political order—coincides with what we defined as basic conformity. But Robson also emphasizes that such commitment by no means implies passive obedience to the decrees of the organs of the welfare state. Our stress on a range of freedom of the micro units points in the same direction. Not only are they expected jointly to stipulate the macro goals, but it is their privilege to evaluate the goal adequacy of the measures proposed, and to establish a common universe of discourse through constructive criticism.

However, the members of a welfare society are at the same time supposed to regard their private interests. This now raises the critical question of whether, and in what manner, those private interests can be reconciled with the public interest, earlier revealed by instrumental analysis as the requirement of quasi stability.

The answer leads us back to the very outset of our inquiry, where we tried to demonstrate that the persistence of the micro units and their enduring freedom crucially depend on the quasi stability of the macro order to which they belong. Thus we arrive at the conclusion that *the true private interest is identical with the public interest.*

In the face of such coincidence it is quite puzzling why the micro units should ever deviate from the stabilizing path, pursuing subsidiary, merely transitory, and even contrary interests with destabilizing consequences. In trying to solve this puzzle, we shall once more encounter the distorting effect that the structure of late capitalism has on the behavior of the micro units, and also the need for planning if the public, and with it the true private, interest is to be satisfied after all.

PLANNED ADJUSTMENT OF PRIVATE TO PUBLIC INTEREST

There are two preconditions for a member of a welfare society to act spontaneously in accord with his or her true interest. He or she must *know concretely* what this interest is in a given situation, and must be *willing* to act accordingly. Remembering the organizational and technological structure of organized capitalism, it is easy to understand why, as a rule, either condition is absent, so that ignorance of what adequate behavior consists in, but also unwillingness to adopt it, predominates.

It is noteworthy that the *problem of ignorance* hardly ever arose during the liberal era. Again the socioeconomic realm provides an illuminating example. The impersonal pressures of scarcity of resources and of unbridled competition, together with resource mobility, created the unequivocal aim of maximizing receipts and minimizing expenditures. This action directive fully satisfied the private interest in economic survival. And in establishing a negative feedback mechanism it eliminated—at least over the medium period of business cycles—any distortions of the macro process.

Compare with such uniformity of behavior *the multiplicity of action directives* and the *uncertainty of expectations* that result from the weakening of the former pressures and the immobilization of human and material resources. No compensatory mechanism any longer reverses the feedbacks that stimulate both inflation and deflation. With an indefinite time horizon of production and investment, even the profit motive has lost determinacy; and the private interest, as conceived by the economic factors, deteriorates into unpredictable strategies aiming at security or expansion.

However, even if in certain situations an average marketer is fully aware of his or her true interest and the conduct suitable to pursuing it, *excessive risks* may check their *willingness* to act accordingly. A typical example is the strategy usually applied by ordinary firms at the bottom of a recession. The only step suitable to starting recovery is a rise in output. But no individual producer will take this step in isolation, because he or she cannot know in advance whether an increase of supply will meet with a complementary increase in demand. We have here another instance of the "solidarity principle," which we met in discussing spontaneous investment as a cure for technological unemployment. Also in the present case, only a simultaneous rise in output on the part of a segment of producers of different commodities or a spontaneous rise of aggregate demand will create another circuit of buyers and sellers that ensures the profitability of output expansion. But in an uncontrolled market there is no intrasystemic incentive for either stimulus. A revival can be expected with certainty only from an act of planning, namely, an increase of aggregate demand through public spending.

Similar risks make all investment decisions a gamble in the prevailing regime of *administered prices*. As these no longer reflect the actual supply-demand conditions, excess capacities and underinvestment abound. But it is not only avoidance of investment risks that turns growing numbers of producers to the pursuit of short-term interests. In view of the uncertainty of the future, they aim at an equivalent of what in the sphere of consumption has been denounced as instant gratification.

SOCIAL LEARNING AND MANIPULATIVE CONTROLS

What are the possibilities for countering those destructive behavioral tendencies—destructive for the system at large, and for that reason also for the emancipatory potential of individual action? Fortunately we need not think only of public initiative. The history of capitalism is rich with examples of small groups inspired by anticipating insight, who overcame the initial resistance of large majorities through the persuasive power of the enlightened word, spoken and written. Instances are the steady advance in social legislation, collective bargaining, progressive taxation, and, more recently, the fiscal and monetary controls of Keynesian provenance. All those measures must be judged as *emancipatory achievements of the past that retain their validity* side by side with the reforms advocated here.

As a consequence, we can attribute to the welfare state, as it has developed up to the present, the following four functions:

1. It provides *social security* in the widest sense at the micro level. This includes all forms of social insurance, the "safety net" of entitlements, and subsidies to agriculture, to some sunset industries, and even to individual enterprises in distress.

2. It tries to control the economic process at large with the prime aim of *stabilization through reducing industrial fluctuations*.

3. It tries to *regulate business behavior*, partly to make up for the dwindling power of competition and partly in order to protect the environment.

4. It expands the productive activity of the public domain in order to *provide substitute employment*.

In the present context, monetary and fiscal controls as instruments of stabilization are of special interest, because of the manner in which they *manipulate microbehavior without enforcing it*. They do so by opening and closing profit opportunities through public spending, tax policy, and regulation of the interest rate, leaving a wide range for spontaneous response. But for that very reason the response may not be goal-adequate. It will be so only if the purpose of such controls is *understood and approved by the micro units*.

For this reason the role of *social learning* cannot be overestimated. This was demonstrated when, during the New Deal era, government tried to stimulate private investment, and thus employment, through public works. The policy failed because business reacted by curtailing private investment—partly out of a mistaken fear of inflation but mainly as a protest against what was seen as an illegitimate intervention. A generation later the response was positive and has remained so—not least as the result of the *enlightened teaching* that business leaders have since received in the progressive schools of business administration.

The example is instructive in a wider context. It tells us that there are *no strict psychological mechanisms* which would make the response of the micro units to a public stimulus easily predictable. A tax reduction may, but need not, raise private spending, nor will a tax increase necessarily curtail it. Therefore, in critical situations manipulative controls may have to be supplemented by enforcement of behavior—in the above instances by taxing unspent purchasing power or by blocking the liquidation of assets, respectively.

There is a special field in which, in the absence of controls, actions violating the public interest are likely to prevail: *the setting of administered prices and wages*. It has long been maintained that a reserve army of unemployed is indispensable for the proper functioning of a market economy, so as to prevent wages from being pushed beyond the value of the marginal product of labor. Our discussion of cost-push inflation and the ensuing wage-price spiral has confirmed this fear, and no reform scheme can succeed unless it offers an antidote.

The problem is one of simple arithmetic. Stability can be maintained only so long as the aggregate of wages, profits, interest, and rent, of the claims of government including transfer payments, does not exceed the total of net national output. Public measures of varying severity have been advocated to assure such a balance. Among them the manipulative measures of a so-called *incomes policy* interfere least with the self-determination of the market partners. The general principle consists in rewarding or penalizing employers with subsidies or taxes, respectively, according to whether they keep wages below, or raise them above, a stipulated norm. Under certain conditions employers may be willing to put up with the penalty of a tax. For this reason direct wage and price controls cannot be ruled out once and for all.

OVERCOMING THE UNCERTAINTY OF EXPECTATIONS

As we stated before, behavior of major private organizations will be discussed in the next chapter. But at this point we must not pass over a possible corrective of destabilizing behavior as shown by the members of the private power structure. To the extent to which monopolization and administering of prices and wages result from the uncertainty of future developments, the question arises of *whether such uncertainty of expectations cannot be reduced* by appropriate methods of planning. In fact, overcoming such uncertainty may well be a prime task of public control.

The first step in this direction would be to give *detailed information to the public about the goals of reform and the successive private actions required to attain them*. But such communications will elicit adequate micro behavior only if their content is accepted as true. Leaving aside measures we discussed earlier, such as monetary and fiscal controls or an incomes policy, confidence at the micro level will be established only if the planning authorities will supplement and, if necessary, even supplant private actions with specific public actions, in particular with a *standby program of public investment and consumption*. In all likelihood such a stockpile, which can be activated at short notice, would fulfill its function by its mere presence. It would bestow on the expectations of the micro units a degree of certainty that should induce them spontaneously to pursue the stabilizing path.

There is a silent assumption underlying this plea for public control of private behavior: the assumption that *the public agents will themselves behave in a goal-adequate manner*. But is it not a fundamental principle of the postabsolutist era that we should be ruled by a government of law and not of men?

Taken literally, this principle has always been a fiction, because it is men who interpret the law. Yet this does not alter the fact that extension of the "rule of men" appears inseparable from a system in which impersonal constraints are steadily weakening. It was Abraham Lincoln who, more than a century ago, raised the grave question of whether a government not too strong for the liberties of the people can be strong enough to maintain its existence in great emergencies. The same question has a wider bearing today. Even in the absence of emergencies, controls by government and large private agencies are bound to interfere with individual self-determination. And not all those controls remove barriers to social and economic equity, especially when we think of the scope of executive power in large-scale business and labor.

In frankly acknowledging this state of affairs, we point to the power that will ultimately determine the range of our freedom. We restate it in the form of the ancient query: Who will control our controllers?—the next step in our inquiry.

8   Behavior in the Public Domain: Controlling the Controllers

BUREAUCRATIZATION AND MODERN SOCIETY

Awareness of the dangers that the rapidly growing bureaucratic organization of Western society, public as well as private, poses to the liberties of the ordinary citizen is widespread. After all, the decontrolling counterattack on the welfare state draws much of its strength from the promise of banning this danger. But the solution it holds out is a merely negative one—breaking up large parts of the public segment of the administrative body, and drastically limiting the functions of what is left. We are invited to return the public functionaries to the role of "night watchmen" they were expected to play during the liberal era. At the same time we should leave unchecked the vast bureaucracies of the private domain, which have replaced the former competitive order.

So as to arrive at a solution more in accord with the structure of modern society, we must, first of all, dispel some myths. One concerns the present *range of bureaucratic organization*. Contrary to a widely held opinion, civilian government is neither its main locus nor, at least in the United States, its place of origin. It extends today over the entire political, socioeconomic, and cultural spectrum—from governmental agencies, the military establishment, business corporations, trade unions, and professional associations to the churches and the educational institutions.

As far as the *origin* of the modern forms of bureaucracy is concerned, in Europe it leads back to the age of absolutism and thus to governmental organization. But it is noteworthy that it was the demand for a standing army and its financial requirements that gave the initial impetus. In the United States, on the other hand, it was the business corporation that took precedence, followed by military and, not before the New Deal, by civilian administration.

This is not to deny that governmental bureaucracy has everywhere grown by leaps and bounds during this century. But there another myth obscures understanding by imputing this development to the welfare state. In fact, of the roughly 3 million civil servants employed by the executive branch of the U.S. federal government, less than 20 percent provide services of a welfare nature. Even President Johnson's Great Society program raised total federal employment by less than 5 percent.

The confusion is due to the fact—discussed in another context—that *expenditures* on social welfare at their climax had risen to half the federal budget. But this has by no means led to a proportionate growth of the *manpower* that administers those vast sums. A breakdown of the statistics of federal employment reveals the true reason for the bureaucratic expansion: U.S. involvement in four wars during the present century. This has inflated not only the directly defense-related departments but, as a consequence of the economic mobilization inseparable from modern warfare, the entire governmental setup. Persistent international tensions have perpetuated this development during the periods of uneasy peace.

GOVERNMENT AS A SUBJECT AND AS AN OBJECT OF CONTROL

In trying to assess the scope and the limits of authority of those controllers, we must distinguish between the administrative heads and the corps of subordinates. Speaking first of the heads, we meet them in a twofold role: as subjects and as objects of control. In the former capacity they are supposed to supervise the administrative apparatus and to assure the legality and efficiency of its operation. We shall presently examine this function more closely. But it will be instructive to begin with the manner in which the leaders are themselves controlled.

Starting with the *governmental setup*, we must distinguish between presidential and parliamentary regimes. In the former it is only the chief executive who is subject to external control—every four years by the majority vote of the electorate that chooses him, and legislatively, in the U.S. Constitution, by an adverse vote of a two-thirds majority of both houses of Congress. The lower heads of administration are appointed by the chief executive and are subject, after senatorial confirmation, to his exclusive and continuous control. This, at least, is the presumption—which, however, is greatly modified in practice. Considering the number of department heads in a modern state, the multiplicity and diversity of functions, and, especially in times of emergency, the need for prompt action, those subheads enjoy a high degree of autonomy. Such autonomy extends even to the lower echelons if the senior posts are filled by political appointees who automatically change when a different administration takes over. The mere fact of such temporal limitation strengthens the authority of the permanent bureaucracy.

Contrary to appearances, its discretion is no less wide in a parliamentary regime, where the heads of the administrative departments, along with the chief executive, are normally members of the legislative body and as such are elected by popular vote. In principle, such a regime permits the majority party, and thus indirectly the voters it represents, to control the leaders from day to day. But in practice such control confines itself to broad outlines of policy framing, leaving the implementation to the administrative body.

Such wide discretion of the administrative leaders is hardly a novelty; it was no different during the liberal era, except that their range of activity was much more narrowly circumscribed. What is novel is the huge bureaucratic apparatus with the help of which the leaders now discharge their duties. At first sight its members enjoy little autonomy of their own, because of the hierarchic order of every bureaucracy. But again, with the ever growing complexity of the regulatory tasks, at least the higher echelons administer in a large measure according to their own devices.

A word must be added about control in the handling of *foreign affairs*. This has always been a field in which executive power ruled supreme. According to the British Constitution, it is the king or queen who, on the advice of the ministers, not only concludes treaties but also declares war—a decision that can be revoked only *ex post facto* by a majority vote of Parliament overthrowing the government.

In sharp contrast, the U.S. Constitution obligates the president to conclude treaties "by and with the advice and consent of the Senate," whereas the power to declare war is the prerogative of Congress. The latter mandate, ostensibly a unique departure from Western tradition, in fact confirms the rule, considering the many transgressions that, under the weight of "operational compulsion" (a phrase used by Arthur M. Schlesinger) have occurred since the early years of the Republic.

Perhaps the most striking transgression was John F. Kennedy's handling of the Cuban missile crisis. But his example is also proof that, in the atomic age, a crisis that threatens the physical existence of the nation cannot be resolved by debates in a legislative body. On the other hand, the events surrounding the conduct of the Vietnam War bear ample testimony to the dangers of an "imperial presidency." The conclusion to be drawn from either experience defines as the predominant task of foreign policy, in this day and age, the timely recognition of an evolving crisis and the prudent application of all means available to avert it. Even if accompanied occasionally by ugly noises, both superpowers have done so in recent decades, in the absence of any statutory control and aided by a sane public opinion. How safe is this check?

BUSINESS EXECUTIVES AS SUBJECTS AND AS OBJECTS OF CONTROL

Turning now to the main analogue of governmental leadership in the *nongovernment sphere*—business executives—we must take into account a structural change that occurred during the present century. It has sometimes been said that Marx, were he returned to life, would be shocked to find his revolutionary proletariat transformed into a petty bourgeoisie fully conscious that it has more to lose than its chains. He would be no less surprised at the modern embodiment of his "capitalist." Big business has far outdistanced the small and medium-sized enterprises of his time—in the United States, of about 13 million proprietorships, some 2 million are incorporated, earning almost 90 percent of the receipts of all firms.

Of those corporations a mere 0.40 percent, with assets of more than $100 million each, hold more than 70 percent of all corporate wealth, while the share of the entire corporate sector in national income amounts to roughly one-half.

It stands to reason that the mere size of large corporations implies a complex hierarchical structure, and thus a bureaucratic setup unknown in the "free enterprises" of the liberal era. In fact, when discussing the concentration and centralization of capital, Marx foresaw such a development. What he could not foresee was the change in the tasks of management and, as a consequence, in the human type of managers. It is true, as the above figures show, that Marx's "capitalist" has by no means disappeared, and his contribution to employment, as distinguished from output, is still quite considerable. But as "entrepreneur" he has been relegated to the backstage, and in the context of business "control" our attention must center on the large enterprises.

It is significant that, even within these corporations, the executives have more recently undergone a profound transformation when compared with the generation of business leaders who set large-scale enterprise on the map a century ago. Those men still displayed attitudes and practices of the liberal entrepreneur, though raised to the monumental; they certainly were anything but bureaucrats. In fact, names like Rockefeller, Carnegie, Harriman, and Morgan acquired an almost mystical quality as symbols of an entire cultural period. In contrast, today the man in the street would be embarrassed if he had to name the chief exeuctive of, say, General Motors, General Electric, or United States Steel. The flamboyant tycoons of the past have been replaced by colorless professionals, the majority of whom rose to the top neither from "rags" nor from family connections, but from lower administrative positions, often based on science and technology. Half a century ago most business leaders were still trained on the job and had little professional education. Today almost all have gone to college, and a third hold a graduate degree, with business administration a major subject in higher education.

Profound as these structural changes were, they did little to reduce the autonomy of the manager, which had prevailed in the era of nonincorporated business. Though formally subjected to the control of stockholders and boards of directors, so long as they are

successful, they enjoy a degree of independence no political leader
can boast of. They defend such autonomy by pointing to the anonymous forces of competition that, they claim, limit their discretion-
ary power to what serves the general welfare. This was indeed a
weighty argument during the liberal era and has acquired new validity internationally. But domestically a regime of oligopoly and
fix-prices largely refutes this claim, and the much maligned increase in governmental regulation of business must be seen as a
substitute, even if not always an effective one, for the impersonal
forces of the market. Moreover, the slogan "get government off our
back" is meant only for prosperous times, as is illustrated by the
cries of Lockheed and Chrysler for emergency support, not to mention the hundreds of millions of dollars in outstanding federal loans
and guarantees to the business community at large.

These last remarks dispel another myth—that of the superiority
of the corporate bureaucracy over the governmental hierarchy in
efficiency, flexibility, and foresight. It seems hardly necessary to
cite specific instances of business "bureaucratization" in the pejor-
ative sense of the term. It would be difficult to find public enterprises and governmental administrations more deficient in innova-
tive spirit or in correctly evaluating their future range of action
than the U.S. steel or machine tool producers.

To sum up, we recognize a strong and growing assimilation on
the part of the governmental and the nongovernmental organizations of Western society with the positive as well as the negative
features of a bureaucratic model. How far such assimilation has
gone is indicated by the ease with which the upper echelons of
business move into leading governmental positions and vice versa.
There is good reason to warn of the dangers that such all-pervading
hierarchical organization of modern life poses. But those dangers
cannot be grasped, let alone fought, unless one is aware of the
indispensable functions that have fallen to public and private administrators in an era of high technology, of ever growing complexity of dispositions, and altogether of an organizational structure designed for the rational adjustment of means to deliberately chosen
ends. Only within this context does the intricate and even contradictory nature of control of the controllers manifest itself.

We have so far stressed the negative function of such control,
intended to limit the free discretion of the controllers. But we must

not forget that such discretion is the source of initiative and pro-ductive innovation. The person who accepts the popular com-plaints of the "routine-mindedness" of bureaucrats—and who would lightly dismiss them—will conceive the task of controlling the con-trollers as one of *making them responsible rather than of limiting their discretion*. Specifically, this means that the public functionaries are to see themselves as guardians of what at the present stage of eman-cipation is the public interest, while the private bureaucracies are to be prompted at least not to counter it. What can we say of suit-able means to those ends?

PARTICIPATION AND DECENTRALIZATION

There seem to be several answers to this question. Two of them can be labeled by the popular terms "*participation*" and "*decentrali-zation*," respectively. "Participation" refers to the opening of ad-ministrative positions to a wider stratum of the population, selected by yardsticks other than those which today determine admission to the status of civil servant or business manager. Decentralization, on the other hand, aims at entrusting administrative responsibility to a wider array of regional, local, and functional representatives.

Either of those demands is meritorious on its own ground. They are basic features of a healthy democracy, and their neglect today is largely responsible for the widespread skepticism with which the prevailing institutions are met. It is, however, quite a different question to what extent realization of those postulates will strengthen control over the controllers.

As far as the quest of *participation* is concerned, a passage from Lenin's *State and Revolution* comes to mind. Surveying the socioec-onomic structure of advanced capitalism, he comes to this conclu-sion: "Accounting and control . . . have become the extraordinary simple operations of watching, recording and issuing receipts, within the reach of anybody who can read, write and knows the first four rules of arithmetic."

Alas, such naive utopianism has been refuted not only by the rise of a highly trained, vast bureaucracy in Lenin's own country but also by the organizational and technological development of the West. The ever more complex forms of know-how and specialized expertise ruling on both sides of the Iron Curtain threaten to generate a new class order dominated by "monopolists of knowledge," a development about which more will be said presently. This condition of modern industrialism sets quite narrow limits to the admission of outsiders into the centers of public and private management. Moreover, can it be taken for granted that such outsiders will be more firmly committed to the public interest than the typical civil servant or business manager? Participation in business administration—"codetermination" of German labor is a good example—must anyhow be limited so long as the risks of enterprise are borne by the owners or the heads of corporations and their stockholders.

The case is no different with *decentralization*. Side by side with the problem of expertise another impediment must be considered. In view of the vital importance of public controls for the stability of the social process, centralization of key operations can hardly be dispensed with. And this all the less so because one cannot take it for granted that the decisions of a multitude of local and sectional bodies will automatically interlock. Their conflicting interests may actually frustrate an effective national policy.

Some observers of the contemporary scene see decentralization develop out of tendencies inherent in the new technology, with the computer creating a new and efficient type of "home industry." Not only, they maintain, will this free the market from the domination of large corporations, but it will integrate economic activity into the general process of living, freeing work from its compulsive features in an industrial regime. Alas, when visualizing the future in the image of the presently ruling power structure, we must conclude that the centralizing tendencies are the ones likely to predominate.

EDUCATION AND SELF-CONTROL

Where else, then, can we find an answer to our question? What we are searching for is a social force capable of molding both the reason and the will of public and private functionaries in accord with their new collective responsibilities. This force can only be *education* in the widest sense of the term.

In approaching this large topic, we must first of all distinguish between *intellectual training* and the *inculcation of standards of action*.

Both types of education have a long history, in the West dating back to the early centuries of the Christian era, when the first "civil service" was formed—the clergy of the Roman church. What is important is the fact that this body was in charge not only of the ecclesiastic establishment but, representing the only *literati*, also administered the affairs of the wordly rulers. Moreover, symbolized in the *Summa* of Thomas Aquinas, the rational and the moral principles taught in the great medieval universities presented themselves in harmonious unity.

With the rise of absolutism a profound change set in that marks administrative schooling to this day. Demand for competent functionaries multiplied, and with it the rise of a secular civil service, emphasizing specialized professional training at the expense of broader cultural indoctrination. The universities remained the training ground. But with the onset of the liberal era they too were transformed into secular institutions. Concern with "values" was relegated to a particular faculty as a subject of knowledge, and education in schools and universities was identified with intellectual instruction.

Progressive democratization strengthened this trend by adopting the merit system for the selection of administrators. No doubt competitive examinations were a great advance over the earlier spoils system, in which loyal supporters of winning politicians were rewarded with public office. And specialized competence, which only the merit system guarantees, is more than ever a requisite of public control.

And yet, with the steadily widening autonomy of public and private functionaries, *more than ever it is personality and character* that ultimately determine the quality of their performance. There, alas, we meet with a wide lacuna in contemporary education. The informal agents of personality formation—family, church, art and literature, the media—speak with conflicting voices. Only at the fringes of modern society—for instance, in the scholastic establishment of the Roman church or in what is left of the tradition of the English public schools, with some spillover to Oxford and Cambridge—do we meet education still concerned with the broadly human.

It may be enlightening to spell out the reason why those borderline institutions succeeded, and in some instances still succeed, where the conventional educational process fails: by integrating the rational with the moral. It is *commitment to a life-ordering principle*. This is obvious where a religious faith inspires the pedagogical enterprise. But as earlier English experience and, in a rather perverted form, even the military academies on the Continent have shown, acceptance of purely secular criteria for "what is done and not done" can instill *loyalty to a self-transcending "whole"*: a nation, a class, a functional group like the army, and, of special importance for our concerns, even a bureaucracy.

What grows out of such commitments—not all of which are compatible with what we understand by emancipation—is the *transformation of control into self-control*. Those older institutions put this to the test by demanding *heavy sacrifices* as the price of admission to the privileges of status, power, and security, which the successful candidate acquires. In the case of the English public schools it was an early separation from the bonds of family life and the pressure to adjust to an artificial kinship system. The Roman cleric, on the other hand, is bound by the vows of obedience, chastity (with emphasis on celibacy), and poverty. It is the mundane objective of those sacrifices to reduce and even efface the private interests of the future public servant—in the extreme case of the cleric, to cut him off from all ties with family and property.

At first sight nothing could be more repugnant to the prevailing spirit in the West than the idea that holding public office, not to say fulfilling other administrative functions, should have to be purchased with self-imposed sacrifice of the private freedoms that are the privilege of any ordinary citizen. And yet, considering the narrow limits of all external checks of which we spoke, self-control of the controllers in a manner appropriate to their new responsibilities remains an essential condition for the protection of our liberties.

A BUREAUCRATIC CLASS?

Having arrived at this conclusion, we realize that Professor Robson's emphasis on an effective welfare society, valid as it is, lacks a complementary prerequisite. It is true that in an industrial society organized as a welfare state, the responsibility and the need for discipline of the ordinary citizen become much greater. But so does *the need for both governmental and private controllers* to be guided by a strong sense of responsibility and by the constraints of self-discipline. More specifically, in a democratic state, in which the maximum of individual self-determination compatible with stability is accepted as an essential aspect of welfare, its guardians must orient their official conduct exclusively to the public interest, and must do so in a spirit of service.

I speak of *official conduct*, pointing to the fact that controllers, like the rest of us living in a stratified society, are "split" into several "selves," each playing its "role." But in contrast with ordinary citizens, whose separate selves on the whole bear a private character, controllers at every level of competence can be defined by the fact that *their socially relevant role is public* and, on principle, must not be influenced by the concerns of their private selves, an inner sanctum they share with everyone else.

We know only too well that such separation of the public and the private self is at best an ideal norm, violation of which forms part of our daily news. But it is not so long ago that what we now regard as a transgression, leading in extreme cases to court action, was treated as an appendage of private privilege. Contrariwise, acknowledgment of an independent public self as the earmark of authentic political leaders and administrators has done much to focus popular attention on the public interest itself.

It is a far distance from a clerical bureaucracy ultimately inspired by a transcendent faith to a body of mundane controllers conscientiously playing their public role. But with secularism dominant and the limitation of all institutional checks and balances, this is all Western man can appeal to in the last resort. Yet even this trust, faint as it may be, may be reduced further when he listens to voices that betray fear of the very *esprit de corps* of our controllers.

I refer to the growing apprehension that what we witness as the outgrowth of a democratic framework is in fact the *formation of a new class*. And the presence of a powerful military-industrial complex, to which we may well add the administrative functionaries, public and private, raises such fears above the level of a wild fantasy.

Perhaps one could give this tendency a less ominous interpretation by relating it to Thorstein Veblen's vision of the approaching rule of the "engineers" of society guided by an "instinct of workmanship," which displaces the dominion of "pecuniary values." And it is not without interest that rudimentary, even if highly controversial, propensities of this kind can be observed in the objectives of some large corporations. For them, promotion of education, building better communities, and protection of the environment have become subsidiary aims. This by no means implies that the lure of pecuniary values, expressing itself in the strength of the profit motive and the commitment to the private ownership and disposal of the means of production, has in any way weakened.

It would at least be premature to accept the formation of a bureaucratic class as a foregone conclusion. So long as the administrative bodies, public and private, recruit their leading personnel on the basis of objective criteria—passing intelligence tests or competing on the basis of professional competence—our controllers lack a main characteristic of a class: *closure*. The ultimate safeguard should, of course, be the viability of representative government. In other words, the bureaucratic corpus can be held in check so long as fundamental decisions are made by people outside the administrative circle and the interest groups allied with it. I leave it to the reader, who has followed the ambivalent conduct of the representative bodies in the United States and England in recent decades, to judge the efficiency of this guardianship of our liberties.

Sober reflection on the countervailing forces at work in shaping behavior in both the private and the public domain must leave some earnest doubt as to whether striving for emancipatory goals, and especially for egalitarian freedom, is a promising enterprise. This thrusts upon us an ultimate question: Is the attempt to bend the course of events in this direction an *obligation* springing from an indisputable imperative irrespective of the prospect of success?

From the outset we have made it clear that our analysis of policies to be pursued and of the behavior patterns to be enlisted in such pursuit is primarily instrumental, that it is devoted to the study of means suitable to attain, or at least to approximate, an *a priori stipulated* end. It is this a priori that we shall now abandon, including the goal itself as an issue that needs to be vindicated.

9 Toward a Communal Ethic

A FIRST COMMANDMENT

In speaking of an "obligation" or an "imperative" to pursue a goal, we step outside the epistemological framework within which our inquiry has so far moved. We no longer dwell in the realm of facts and factual relations, but find ourselves in a region ruled by value judgments and norms. Alas, this is a region in which the modern mind finds it difficult, if not impossible, to reason because, according to the dominant methodology of knowledge, propositions about values and norms cannot be demonstrated intersubjectively. How, then, are we to gain a firm ground for our advocacy of emancipation and its goals?

Before attempting an answer, we must recognize that the range of "unreasonable" propositions is even wider than we have so far indicated. What this refers to has been put into epigrammatic form by Ferdinand Lassalle:

> Point not the goal, until you plot the course,
> For end and means to man are tangled so
> That different means quite different aims enforce;
> Conceive the means as ends in embryo.

Stated in more prosaic terms, we apply value judgments also in the selection of *means*, and this irrespective of their suitability for goal attainment. We become aware of this whenever a suitable act of control conflicts with accepted standards of conduct. This is a source of well-known controversies in planning—for instance, about the range of nationalization of production—controversies that can be resolved only by another value judgment. Do we think it of greater value to strive after a goal, even if we judge the suitable means as "unworthy," than to preserve the integrity of our means evaluation, even if this compels us to abandon the goal? In other words, value criteria for the selection of means must enter into the stipulation of our goals.

In the face of such a broad range of norms, can we perhaps stave off the value dimension after all, by demonstrating that the emancipatory goals are self-evident or, less categorically, universally accepted? That unfortunately this is not so was shown at the very outset of our deliberations, when we had to admit two opposite evaluations of the global revolution of our day—as the road to a New Jerusalem or to anomic self-destruction. And even those who endorse emancipation must acknowledge that its constructive potential rests on some more basic preconditions that themselves are threatened by a destructive potential—mankind must exist and continue to exist at a sociopolitical, intellectual and technological level of civilization that assures self-determination. We thus proclaim as *supreme value* the presence and future of a self-determining humanity—a state of civilization toward which the stages of emancipation, with its advance to egalitarian freedom, are successive approximations?

Modern secularized Westerners may well think so. But they need to be reminded that there were, and still are, vast civilizations whose members deny a supreme value to man's earthly pilgrimage. One may even wonder whether survival of mankind can be accepted as an aspect of supreme value by those Westerners for whom this pilgrimage leads through a valley of tears to man's true destination in afterlife.

Far from being a moot point in the disputes of theologians and philosophers, these divergent beliefs can have far-reaching practical consequences. A person who expects to enter the Christian heaven or the Muslim paradise, or ultimately to be released into nirvana, is much more prone to wage a "just" or "holy" war, even at the risk of nuclear annihilation of mankind, than his or her secular counterpart who believes only in this life.

Nor does this secular counterpart always acknowledge self-determination or freedom as a component of what we have defined as supreme value. It was Bertrand Russell, with his alarming dictum "better Red than dead," who alerted us to a potential conflict between survival and freedom. In whatever manner this dilemma be resolved, what we are wrestling with here are the rudiments of a *communal ethic* as the criterion of action in this third stage of emancipation.

TRADITIONAL AND COMMUNAL ETHICS

What distinguishes a communal ethic from all other forms of ethics that have been handed down to us through millennia is the subject of Hans Jonas's book *The Imperative of Responsibility*, from which I am going to cite some relevant passages. They deal, first of all, with

the commands of traditional ethics, which refer to the direct dealings of man with man to the exclusion of the nonhuman world. At the same time man and his basic condition are considered as constant in essence and not subject to a reshaping technology. The good and evil about which actors have to care lie close to the act and are not matters of remote planning. The ethical universe is composed of contemporaries, and its horizon of the future confined to the foreseeable span of their lives.

It follows that the knowledge required to assure the morality of action is not that of the scientist or the expert, but is available to all men of goodwill. The good or bad of an action is wholly decided within that short-term context—the long run of consequences is left to chance, fate, or providence (free quotation, pp. 4–5).

The limited scope of those traditional postulates fully corresponds to the narrow range that the technologies and ideologies of the past left to human action. But we need only to think of the two existential threats of our own age—atomic war and the ecological perils—to be shocked into awareness of how radically our own world differs from those halcyon days. Neither nature nor mankind at large is safe anymore from man himself, and the *worst evils are now collective misdeeds.*

Not that the commands of traditional ethics have lost their validity. But to the extent to which it is in our power as members of a collectivity to prevent collective misdeeds, *solidarity in fighting avoidable threats to mankind and nature has gained priority.* This is so because the same material and social technologies that empower us to destroy also help us to protect, once we acknowledge the presence and future of a self-determining humanity as our communal responsibility. Citing Hans Jonas once more: *we ought because we can.*

So, indeed, I affirm the preservation of a particular mundane state of affairs as the supreme imperative of an ethic befitting our time. I do so in full awareness that this imperative cannot be derived from observation or from ratiocination. But speaking as a secular Westerner, and speaking first of all to other Westerners who share my basic outlook, I feel justified in basing the imperative that henceforth is to guide our actions on what in rational terms is no more than a working hypothesis.

But need we be so modest? Can we not appeal to a revival of religious sentiment all over the West? In a thought-provoking address Daniel Bell offers at least three recent sprouts of such tendencies with clear ethical implications: a stepping back into tradition, of which a new fundamentalism and the "born again" movement are examples; widespread rejection of all megastructures, supported by the idea of "caritas" as the private exercise of the functions the welfare state has appropriated; and a revival of mystical modes of thought, reopening the world of the nonrational and with it of the "sacred."

I accept this diagnosis and admit that, in the absence of a true community and during the painful transition to one, the forces to which Professor Bell points may have a therapeutic effect by strengthening the endurance of atomized individuals. But I doubt that those forces can be agents of reintegration, because by their very nature they abet the already spreading tendency of withdrawal into noncommittal privacy. To return to the difference between traditional and communal ethics, I cannot see how on that basis the narrow individual horizon of space and time can be overcome, a transformation on which the integrity of mankind and nature depends.

Perhaps it is true that the consummation of this third stage of emancipation can be achieved only in the spirit of a new religiosity.

But—and here I again agree with Professor Bell—a religion cannot be manufactured, and social integration is not its primary function. Therefore, if at the present stage we search for the precepts of a communal ethic, we must do so within the confines of a secular universe of discourse, admitting that its first principle is a product of "intuition," and thus by rational standards a gamble. But we may also remember the dictum of the English poet Gerard Manley Hopkins, "Intuition is the secular version of faith."

This is not the place for a further elaboration of a communal ethic, nor am I qualified for such a task. One may even wonder whether the time will be ripe for this task before quasi stability has been established, that is, before a viable tomorrow exists. But if this should be so, the reader may well ask what purpose is served by discussing even the nature of a first principle while we are still in the birth throes of a new era.

I answer this question by pointing once more to the open-endedness of the present moment, which confronts us with a bifurcation, if not "multifurcation," of paths into the future. Faced with such ambiguity but also compelled to act, we need a criterion for the decision as to which goal to pursue. Choosing in accord with an ethical imperative frees our choice from arbitrariness, even if the imperative cannot be more than a lodestar. To make it concrete in terms of institutions must be left to those who have safely entered a stable tomorrow.

10   The Prospect of Freedom

So we descend from the lofty heights of philosophical rumination to the stony ground of the contemporary world, carrying with us a compass that can guide the actors in the social process—controllers and controlled—along the goal-adequate path. What is, we ask in conclusion, the prospect that in this way egalitarian freedom will in fact be approximated?

We are now in a position to give a clear, though conditional, answer. If the controllers act wisely and stay within the limits of their functions, and if the controlled adhere to the standards that are in accord with the public interest, by this also satisfying their true private interest, the chances for freedom will be auspicious. In Professor Robsons's terms, after our reform program has been carried out, the imperfect welfare state of today will gain in probity and efficiency, being sustained by a solidary welfare society that in turn is protected by the controls of a reformed welfare state.

And yet two contradictory lessons must be drawn from this inquiry. The first is that striving for a beneficial conjunction of freedom and order is indeed a feasible project. However, a second lesson dampens all sanguine expectations: Transition from the current state of affairs to that propitious future is impeded by obstacles that may well prove insuperable.

In order to arrive at a tentative evaluation of the relative strength of these opposing forces, we shall present a retrospective summary of the main causes of the unstable *status quo*, and also of the obstacles to stabilizing reform. Moreover, we shall venture a guess as to what is likely to happen if those obstacles cannot be overcome.

A SUMMARY OF THE MAIN SOURCES OF INSTABILITY

Let us begin by once more taking stock of the major factors at the root of the present instability. We found the basic cause of the problem in the worldwide breakup of certain natural and sociopolitical constraints of the past—forces of repression from the viewpoint of individual freedom, but at the same time forces of protection from the viewpoint of social stability. Closer examination of the relationship between freedom and stability forced on us the conclusion that in the very interest of enduring freedom, new constraints in the form of planning must take the place of the vanishing ones, thus actualizing the potential for a new stage of emancipation.

In more closely studying the predicaments of the transitional phase through which we are passing, and also the institutional and attitudinal changes necessary to resolve them, we have confined ourselves mainly to the *domestic scene*. We did not do so to belittle the role of international affairs. Quite to the contrary—unless the contest of the superpowers can be kept at the level of stalemate, discussion of domestic reform is pointless. The Damocles sword of atomic war will continue hanging over an ostensibly peaceful world, considering the proliferation of atomic weapons through a malcontent Third World.

It is the *absence of any controlling authority in international relations* that confines a study of planning to intranational relations. In particular, the range of eliciting, guiding, and (in the last resort) of enforcing behavior, and thus of reform, ends at the national border. For the same reason—limits of effective public control—we have concentrated on the nations of the West, with the United States in the foreground.

If we now reexamine the *intranational sources of today's instability*, we do not find it easy to present them in any systematic order, because of the reciprocity of influence of some of these factors. Thus it may be illuminating to begin with two circumstances that have been associated with capitalism from its very beginning: large-scale *unemployment* and substantial social and economic *inequality*. What sets these conditions apart is the fact that their past impact differed greatly from what we are experiencing today. In earlier times their destabilizing effect was greatly mitigated by another feature of the capitalist trend, the steady, autonomous expansion of the private domain. This reduced large unemployment to relatively short periods, at the same time raising the income pyramid as a whole.

This favorable state of affairs no longer prevails, a fact that many observers trace to a fall in the rate of growth of output in the established industrial countries, itself a consequence of falling productivity. Contrariwise, we see in those changes only passing difficulties, which will be overcome by what is otherwise the true source of our troubles. I refer to the *ongoing technological revolution*, which is bound to raise productivity again, and with it the growth of aggregate output. But, to quote the Organization for Economic Cooperation and Development, it may well be *"jobless growth."* In other words, the new technology in its various forms should set all qualms about productivity to rest. But at the same time, it makes *technological unemployment and its compensation* a major issue of stabilization.

We have demonstrated in great detail that there is no "self-regulating mechanism" in an uncontrolled market that could achieve such compensation, and thus prevent downward cumulation of economic activity as a whole. We found the critical stumbling block in the *excessive risks* that new investment, the only factor capable of compensation, faces in the absence of solidary action among potential investors. Indeed, this impediment—a structural weakness of any uncontrolled market—hampers investment quite generally, unless a prior rise in demand provides a guiding price signal.

In fact, this strategic signal has been widely eliminated by another destabilizing change, the *self-organization of producers* on both sides of the social fence. Expressing itself in administered wages and prices, it paralyzes the stabilizing feedbacks prevailing in a competitive market. The consequence is growing uncertainty of buyers and sellers about the tendency of market movements, resulting in a profusion of incompatible behavior patterns.

Earlier we gave the reason why our list of "destabilizers" is limited to intranational factors. An exception needs to be made for the economic development in certain areas of the Third World. By at-

tracting capital and know-how from the West, this process not only
deprives the latter of essential resources, and thus of employment
opportunities, but also exposes it to the competition of those newly
industrializing regions.

So far we have concentrated on *instability* due to structural unemployment in an uncontrolled market. Moreover, a permanent and
possibly rising reserve army of idle workers is likely also to be a
new source of *inequality*. Constant pressure on wages, combined
with the traditional sexual and racial blocks, is intensifying social
tension. If we take into account the superiority that specialized
knowledge and expertise bestow on the managing minority of the
approaching "computer society," Disraeli's gloomy vision of "two
nations" may now take shape in potentially rich societies.

A MINIMUM PROGRAM OF REFORM

As an antidote we have offered a *minimum program of reform* to
reduce both instability and inequity to tolerable levels, first of all
by overcoming long-term structural unemployment. This is to be
achieved by counteracting the *consequences* of the destabilizing factors rather than by removing those factors themselves. To some
extent such a removal would be practically impossible, as is the
case with the rigidified structure of organized capitalism or the industrial growth outside the national borders of the West. In another instance—forestalling the progress and the dispersion of the
new technology—even if it were possible, would be highly unde-
sirable in view of the demographic development.

The institutional changes proposed for the establishment of maximum employment can be subsumed under the heading "*expanding
the public domain*." This agrees not only with the views of other
observers but also with the shifting balance between the private
and the public domains. Our plan differs to the extent to which
the measures proposed will fill some wide gaps in the present activity of late capitalism. It emphasizes the open employment opportunities in a greatly *deficient infrastructure*, and also the neglect of
nonmaterial goods and services, activities for which we have chosen
the label "*planned domestic colonization*." In other words, the new
employment opportunities are not seen as makeshift public works,
the direct benefit of which is often quite doubtful. Rather, such

"colonization" is to raise the Western societies, which wrongly boast about their developmental achievements, to a higher level of civilization.

It so happens that the public services thus newly provided offer special chances to female labor, thus contributing to sexual equalization, while they are at the same time least harmful to the environment. Combined with an incomes policy as a safeguard against inflationary tendencies of maximum employment, and with educational measures that preclude a "class monopoly of knowledge," such a program should go a long way toward reintegrating the Western nations.

To an outsider such a program might appear as the fruit of common sense, likely to gain universal approval irrespective of party affiliation, economic status, or philosophical viewpoint. But from the outset we stressed the presence of possibly insuperable *obstacles*. Those obstacles are not located in any objective barrier to the institutional transformation as such. The true obstacle is the *refusal of an apparent majority of the Western public* to accept the precondition for such transformation: *the broadening and strengthening of the functions of the welfare state.*

We also must not forget that the very presence of instability offers advantages to certain power groups that profit from the rigidification of the socioeconomic structure. Nor are those groups on principle opposed to "planning." Instead, the rivalry of private and public controllers opens a new source of destabilization, with private control espoused in the name of freedom.

Still, such groups could hardly carry the day at the voting booth, were they not supported by the conventional wisdom of an electorate that accepts the principles of laissez-faire and of the "night-watchman state" as articles of faith. Nowhere is this dogma more powerful than in the United States with its long tradition of distrust of government and a failure to perceive the public domain as the guardian of a viable private domain. What this amounts to is well illustrated by the ambivalent attitude toward the welfare state on the part of Congress and the general public.

When speaking earlier of the specific policies of the welfare state, we stressed four functions of public control: at the micro level, social security in the widest sense; at the macro level, economic stabilization; regulation of business behavior; and provision of substitute employment in the public domain. When the Reagan administration took over, it seemed at first that the radical opponents of the welfare state were about to eliminate public controls altogether through a stringent budget policy. However, when the actual attempt was made drastically to reduce expenditures for all types of social insurance, including entitlements, almost unanimous resistance of both parties in Congress made it clear to those spearheading the "Reagan revolution" that the welfare state as guardian of social security is here to stay. In practice the same proved true with regard to the second function, economic stabilization. Notwithstanding the slogans of a *"supply*-side" theory, the actual measures taken—tax reductions and public works in the form of huge rearmament—were the orthodox weapons in the Keynesian arsenal of planned expansion of aggregate *demand*.

On the other hand, the decontrolling zeal directs itself against the third and fourth functions enumerated above. No fair-minded observer would want indiscriminately to defend bureaucratic interference with the decision making of business. But any wholesale abolition of such regulations is bound to strengthen the existing power structure, and thus the rigidity of market relations. Finally, opposition to government as employer of last resort sees in a permanent reserve army of idle workers a desirable objective rather than a major cause of instability.

IS "MUDDLING THROUGH" A SOLUTION?

These experiences raise a more fundamental question: Can such "muddling through" between reform and reaction maintain itself for long? The answer can only be speculative, because it depends on a trend of events that can be foreseen only imperfectly. What, however, can be foreseen is the strengthening of forces that tend toward further destabilization.

We repeatedly emphasized that we are only at the beginning of a technological revolution, the full displacement effect of which will show only after a nationwide dispersion in plants and offices. We must also expect further growth of the industrial potential of certain regions of the Third World, progressively interfering with output and employment in the West. Nor can we at this point disregard a development that characterizes the United States in particular, and that will sharpen a threatening distributional struggle.

I am referring to the long-term consequences of the steadily rising public debt. Not only is this debt to some extent owed "outside the family"—namely, to foreigners whose capital flow has partly financed successive budgets, thus transforming interest payments into tributes that will diminish the domestically disposable national product. But even the intranational indebtedness is more harmful than the popular slogan that we "owe the debt to ourselves" makes it appear. Those who must pay the taxes to finance interest payments on the national debt are, as a social group, by no means identical with the recipients.

All in all, I fear that, after a prolonged period of "muddling through," what is left of spontaneous conformity will have evaporated. In an earlier context I drew a comparison between the destabilization of modern society and the disintegration of the medieval hierarchy into the rival factions of the "estates of the realm." The outcome was the absolute monarchy—it may now be *another form of autocracy*.

Before pursuing this idea a little further, we should at least briefly make good on an earlier promise to evaluate a phenomenon that once before transformed the self-destructive attitude of an entire nation into solidary identification with the public interest. I refer, of course, to England in 1940, and quite generally to *catastrophe as a catalyst*.

For reasons that hardly need elaboration, war among the great powers can never again have this salutary effect. But there are civilian emergencies, such as runaway inflation or mass unemployment on the order of the Great Depression, that one might expect to open the consciousness of the public to its true interest. Alas, in contrast with the national solidarity that war could achieve when it was still a feasible instrument of politics, those civilian disasters might well prove divisive, considering the difference in the severity with which they are likely to hit different strata. Rather than inspiring solidarity, they may aggravate conflicts of interest, and thus be further stimuli for imposing conformity by autocratic means.

Perhaps one might want to draw a more optimistic conclusion from the effect that the atomic catastrophe in Chernobyl had on public opinion in western Europe. The actions so far taken or planned inspire little confidence. And this above all because Chernobyl has taught us that the peaceful use of atomic energy is compatible with national security only *if it is controlled internationally*—at this stage a utopian imperative.

THE ALTERNATIVE OF AUTOCRACY

Evaluation of modern forms of *autocracy* is rendered difficult because of the overwhelming experience with totalitarianism, an experience that is not only fully documented by its victims but also has been forcefully pictured in George Orwell's novel *1984*. Still we should not forget that almost two decades before Orwell the image of another type of autocracy was given artistic expression in Aldous Huxley's *Brave New World*. Most likely the reader will ask what political significance can be attributed to a literary fantasy over against the reality of a large part of the real world. He or she may be shocked when I answer that Huxley's anticipatory vision seems to me more relevant for perceiving the future of Western man than the actualities of totalitarianism.

In all those actualities, *terror* is the ultimate instrument for enforcing conformity, thus stabilizing not only the social process but also the dominion of its rulers. Workable over a limited period, brutally enforced conformity is, as experience shows, not tolerated indefinitely, though it may take sophisticated hypocrisy and even the passing of generations to make resistance effective.

No such horrors mar the image of Huxley's Great Ford and his partisans. Their rule is based on *universal pleasure*. A general mood of shallow happiness is created by the gratification of man's elementary needs, by unlimited sexual freedom and permanent security of status. There, of course, we have the other side of the coin—such status is to be assigned to every human being even before his or her life begins. With the help of genetic control, psychoactive drugs, and all the tricks of subliminal psychology, not only are the overt actions of the "planned" humans determined, but also all aspects of their consciousness: desires, judgment, and choices. The result is an inegalitarian enslavement that establishes a new and stable hierarchy, in which every social function is performed by a preconditioned executant. And to crown everything, the subjects thus conditioned are made fully content with their lot—"I am really awfully glad that I am a Gamma"—even enjoying a false sensation of freedom.

One may say that there is no empirical order that even comes near to this weird fantasy. And yet must we not admit that, during the half-century since the publication of Huxley's book, technological and cultural changes have occurred that point in that direction?

Recombinant DNA technology, in vitro fertilization, experiments with cloning, and the subliminal influence that the media and Madison Avenue exert not only on our market behavior but also on our choices in the voting booth, not to forget the revolution in sexual mores—where are the limits to mass production of bodies and minds?

There is hope that the Western tradition of individualism, perverted as it is today by its ignoring communal bonds, is still strong enough to resist this trend. Still, if muddling through, not to speak of further decontrolling steps into the past, undermines stability to the point where progressive reform can no longer muster democratic mass support, the welfare state itself may assume autocratic features. Instead of being buttressed by an aware and disciplined welfare society, its political and bureaucratic organs will impose such standards of behavior as they consider appropriate. At its best an analogy might be drawn with the enlightened absolutism of some central European nations two centuries ago or—perhaps the mildest form—Bismarck's constitution for Germany. In such a *Rechtsstaat* a fair degree of private freedom might be granted, but public freedom would have to be surrendered. To invert a phrase used earlier, even *under the most lenient autocratic regime the price of stability would be the loss of self-government.*

EPILOGUE

Nothing of what has above been said about conceivable trends is meant as a prediction. From the outset we stressed the speculative nature of these deliberations. They point to certain potentialities whose strength, however, cannot be judged from the viewpoint of today. But, what is more important, does this reservation not raise a *query about our entire procedure*?

What distinguishes such speculations from the apodictic manner in which we can assert matters of fact or deductive conclusions is a large element of futurity in their content. But is not our inquiry as a whole—our advocacy of progressive planning or our expectation of a nationwide dispersion of automation accompanied by large-scale technological unemployment—based on premises that contain such future-related elements? Did we not in every instance envisage the terminus of a process of which we know only the early phase through which we are passing today?

The problem is related to, though not identical with, an issue that arises at the outset of every scientific investigation. The first step is always the choice of the phenomena that are to form the raw material for the subsequent rational effort. Joseph Schumpeter has given special attention to this issue in his *History of Economic Analysis*. He speaks there of a "preanalytic cognitive act" that he calls a *vision*, a term we ourselves have used several times in comparable connotations. And no doubt the truth of the subsequent derivations depends on the accuracy of the underlying vision. Fortunately there are many situations unaffected by the flow of time, so that the accuracy of the vision can be checked indirectly by testing the rational conclusions. Alas, no such test is available whenever the vision and what is derived from it extends into the future.

Detrimental to knowledge as this impediment is, it is aggravated by another influence. I refer to a bias that from the outset may distort any vision—a bias to which Marx gave the label of *"ideology."* With this term he wanted to point to certain prejudices of the observer: personal makeup, national and social environment, and, above all, rank in the prevailing class structure. Such prejudices are likely to make him or her see what they see in a false light, and may blind them to essential aspects.

So we must indeed ask, How can our reasoning be valid once we acknowledge, as we must, the presence of such future-related elements and the uncertainty they create? It can be valid only if it subjects itself to three limitations: *of temporal range, of the order of magnitude of any planned changes*, and *of the "tone" in which any program of reform is advocated*. Have we taken those limitations into account in our deliberations?

In directing our proposals to the aim of accomplishing no more than a *viable tomorrow*, we have confined them to the first step on which further advances toward the ultimate goal depend. The task of discovering the next steps and the deliberate changes those steps will require have been left to tomorrow's thinkers and actors.

As to the second limitation, it stands to reason that the future-related uncertainties and the risks they create in today's planning grow in proportion to the scope of transformation and the rigidity of the new institutional structure. Therefore, *incremental procedures* must take precedence. They permit us to test the plan's outcome at short intervals and thus make revisions possible, conditions that our major proposals fulfill. What we had to say about foreign and military policy at the present atomic stalemate fits well into an incremental strategy. So does a policy of domestic colonization as a major promoter of maximum employment.

Finally, I have not hesitated to reject the interpretation of the global revolution of our age as either "posthistorical" utopia or impending doom. Nor have I refrained from exposing the alleged cure of our ills offered by the decontrollers as a dangerous illusion. But I have at the same time acknowledged both constructive and destructive tendencies in what may, but need not, be an emancipatory process, thus avoiding any doctrinaire simplification of an extremely complex phenomenon. It is true that, by briefly deviating from the factual to the normative level of inquiry, I have tried to legitimate the ultimate goal, in the service of which my practical proposals have been conceived, as in accord with the first principle of a communal ethic. But I have also admitted that there is no rational argument that will convert those who are prepared to pay the price of destruction that rejection of such an ethic is likely to exact.

I cannot help admitting that, in spite of the pains I have taken to present a balanced account, the ensuing overall picture is far from bright. Perhaps we can brighten it if we exchange our role as involved participants for the detached view of the historian. Whatever the nature of the approaching era and the scope of freedom it will grant, if we escape nuclear annihilation, this will not be the end of history. In this connection we do well to remember that in the past, ancient and modern, freedom asserted itself only in the later stages of an epoch and not at its inception. Such a reminder must certainly not weaken our efforts. But it can sustain our hopes even if we are not fully satisfied with our own accomplishments.

For Further Reading

Ch. 1   Isaiah Berlin, *Four Essays on Liberty*. Oxford: Oxford University Press, 1969.

Pierre Abélard, *Dialectic*, in Cousin, Victor, ed., *Oeuvre inédit d'Abélard*. Paris, 1836.

Sir Geoffrey Vickers, *Human Systems Are Different*. London: Harper & Row, 1983.

Jacob Klein, "The Problem of Freedom," in *Lectures and Essays*. Annapolis: St. John's College Press, 1985.

Ch. 2   R. W. Carlyle and A. J. Carlyle, *A History of Medieval Political Theory in the West*. New York and London: 1903–1936.

Adolph Lowe, "Nationalism and the Economic Order," in *Nationalism*, a report of the Royal Institute of International Affairs. Oxford: Oxford University Press, 1939.

Ch. 3   Winston Churchill, *The Second World War*, vol. III.

Robert L. Heilbroner, *The Nature and Logic of Capitalism*. New York: W. W. Norton & Co., 1985.

Daniel Bell, *The Cultural Contradictions of Capitalism*. New York: Basic Books, Inc., 1976.

Ch. 4   Thucydides, *The History of the Peloponnesian War*, translated and edited by Benjamin Jowett. Oxford: Oxford University Press,

The sequence in which the references are listed corresponds to the sequence in which the respective topics are discussed in the text.

1900.

Jean Jacques Rousseau, *The Social Contract*. Everyman's Library, New York: E. P. Dutton & Co., Inc., 1935.

Adolph Lowe, *The Price of Liberty*. London: The Hogarth Press, 1937; revised 1948.

Fred Clarke, *Education and Social Change*. London 1940.

John Stuart Mill, *On Liberty*. London: The Thinker's Library, 1859.

Wilhelm von Humboldt, *Ideen zu einem Versuch, die Grenzen der Wirksamkeit des Staats zu bestimmen*. Berlin, Deutsche Bibliotek, 1922.

Max Scheler, "Der Geist und die ideellen Grundlagen der Demokratien der grossen Nationen," in *Nation und Weltanschauung*. Leipzig: Deu Neue Geist-Verlag, 1923.

Thomas Mann, "Gedanken in Kriegszeiten," in *Die neue Rundschau*. 1914.

Ch. 5   McGeorge Bundy et al., "The President's Choice." *Foreign Affairs*, Winter 1984–85.

Lester C. Thurow, *The Zero-Sum Society*. New York: Basic Books, 1980.

John Kenneth Galbraith, *The Affluent Society*. Boston: Houghton Mifflin Company, 1958.

Ch. 6   Klaus Haefner, *Mensch und Computer im Jahre 2000*. Basel, Boston: Birkhäuser Verlag, 1984.

Emil Lederer, *Technical Progress and Unemployment*. London: P. S. Kingson, Ltd., 1938.

Adolph Lowe, "Technological Unemployment Reexamined," in L. Eisermaun, ed., *Wirtschaft und Kultursysteme*. Zurich, Eugen Rentsch Verlag, 1955.

Harald Hagemann and Peter Kalmbach, eds., *Technischer Fortschritt und Arbeitslosigkeit*. Frankfurt/New York: Campus Verlag, 1983.

Eileen Appelbaum, "Winners and Losers in the High-Tech Workplace." *Challenge*, Vol. 26, No. 4, 1983.

W. W. Rostow, "Technology and Unemployment in the Western World." *Challenge*, Vol. 26, No. 1, 1983.

Philip Harvey, "Guaranteed Employment as Public Policy."

Unpublished manuscript. New Haven: Center for Studies in Law, Economics and Public Policy, Yale Law School, 1986.

Ch. 7   William A. Robson, *Welfare State and Welfare Society*. London: George Allen & Unwin Ltd., 1976.

Adolph Lowe, *On Economic Knowledge*. 2nd edition, New York/London: M. E. Sharper Inc., 1977.

Ch. 8   Arthur M. Schlesinger, Jr., *The Imperial Presidency*. Boston: Houghton Mifflin Company, 1973.

Thorstein Veblen, *The Instinct of Workmanship and the State of the Industrial Arts*. In *The Tortable Veblen*, ed. Max Lerner. New York: The Viking Press, 1950.

Alwin W. Gouldner, *The Future of Intellectuals and the Rise of the New Class*. New York: Continuum, 1979.

Ch. 9   Hans Jonas, *The Imperative of Responsibility*. Chicago/London: The University of Chicago Press, 1984.

Daniel Bell, "The Return of the Sacred," in *The Winding Passage: Essays and Sociological Journeys*. 1981.

Ch. 10   George Orwell, *1984*. Harmondsworth: Penguin Books, 1949.

Aldous Huxley, *Brave New World*. London: Chatto and Windus, 1932.

Neill Postman, *Amusing Ourselves to Death*. 1985.

Joseph A. Schumpeter, *History of Economic Analysis*. New York: Oxford University Press, 1954.

Thomas Bottomore, ed., *Karl Marx: Early Writings*. 1965.

David A. Stockman, *The Triumph of Politics*. New York: Harper & Row, 1986.

About the Author

ADOLPH LOWE, Emeritus Professor of the Graduate Facility at the New School for Social Research in New York City and of the University of Frankfurt am Main, was born in Stuttgart, Germany in 1893. From 1911 to 1915 he studied law, economics, and philosophy at the Universities of Munich, Berlin, and Tübingen, concluding his studies as Doctor of Law.

From 1919 to 1926 he served as Councillor in the Ministries of Demobilization, Labor and Economics, and as Head of the International Division of the Federal Bureau of Statistics in the Weimar Republic. In 1926 he joined the University of Kiel as Professor of Economic Theory and Sociology and also as Director of Research in the Institute of World Economics. In 1931 as Professor of Economics he moved to the University of Frankfurt am Main, a post from which he was dismissed in 1933.

Between 1933 and 1940 he was Special Honorary Lecturer in economics and political philosophy at the University of Manchester, England. From 1941 to his retirement in 1963 he served as Professor of Economics and also as Director of Research in the Institute of World Affairs at the New School for Social Research. At present he resides in Wolfenbüttel, West Germany.

His major publications include *Economics and Sociology*, *The Price of Liberty*, *The Universities in Transformation*, *On Economic Knowledge*, and *The Path of Economic Growth*. A collection of his major research papers has been published as *Essays in Political Economics*.

Professor Lowe holds two Honorary Doctorates, the Veblen-Commons Award and the Grand Cross of the German Order of Merit.

About the Founder of This Series

RUTH NANDA ANSHEN, Ph.D., Fellow of the Royal Society of Arts of London, founded, plans, and edits several distinguished series, including World Perspectives, Religious Perspectives, Credo Perspectives, Perspectives in Humanism, the Science of Culture Series, the Tree of Life Series, and Convergence. She also writes and lectures on the relationship of knowledge to the nature and meaning of man and to his understanding of and place in the universe. Dr. Anshen's book, *The Reality of the Devil: Evil in Man*, a study in the phenomenology of evil, demonstrates the interrelationship between good and evil. She is also the author of *Anatomy of Evil* and of *Biography of an Idea*. She has lectured in universities throughout the civilized world on the unity of mind and matter and on the relationship of facts to values. Dr. Anshen is a member of the American Philosophical Association, the History of Science Society, the International Philosophical Society and the Metaphysical Society of America.